USS *LAWRENCE*
VS
HMS *DETROIT*

The War of 1812 on the Great Lakes

MARK LARDAS

First published in Great Britain in 2017 by Osprey Publishing,
PO Box 883, Oxford, OX1 9PL, UK
1385 Broadway, 5th Floor, New York, NY 10018, USA
E-mail: info@ospreypublishing.com

Osprey Publishing, part of Bloomsbury Publishing Plc

OSPREY is a trademark of Osprey Publishing, a division of Bloomsbury
Publishing Plc.

A CIP catalog record for this book is available from the British Library

Print ISBN: 978 1 4728 1582 8
PDF e-book ISBN: 978 1 4728 1583 5
ePub e-book ISBN: 978 1 4728 1584 2
XML ISBN: 978 1 4728 2338 0

Index by Rob Munro
Typeset in ITC Conduit and Adobe Garamond
Maps by bounford.com
Originated by PDQ Media, Bungay, UK
Printed in China through World Print Ltd.

17 18 19 20 21   10 9 8 7 6 5 4 3 2 1

Osprey Publishing supports the Woodland Trust, the UK's leading woodland
conservation charity. Between 2014 and 2018 our donations are being spent
on their Centenary Woods project in the UK.

To find out more about our authors and books visit
www.ospreypublishing.com. Here you will find extracts, author interviews,
details of forthcoming events and the option to sign up for our newsletter.

Dedication

This book is dedicated to Peter Rindlisbacher. I have appreciated his art for
many years, and appreciated his advice on this book even more. Even more
delightful, I discovered he is a fellow resident of the Houston metropolitan area.

Author's acknowledgments

No book is the product of the author alone. This one, more than many, was
the result of the assistance of others. First and foremost, I need to thank
Professor Kevin Crisman and Professor Glen Grieco of the Center for
Maritime Archaeology and Conservation at Texas A&M University, who
unselfishly provided advice and illustrations. Walter Rybka and Linda Bolla of
the Erie Maritime Museum also helped with questions about the ships of the
Lakes. Frank Gogos, Curator of the Royal Newfoundland Regiment, provided
information and images about that regiment, which served as marines during
the War of 1812. Major John R. Grodzinski of the Department of History,
The Royal Military College of Canada provided insights on the Canadian and
British side of the conflict. Peter Rindlisbacher, a noted maritime artist, helped
me avoid some egregious errors in the appearance of the ships. Thanks to all.

Author's note

The following abbreviations indicate the sources of the illustrations used in
this volume: AC – Author's Collection; KC – Image contributed by Professor
Kevin Crisman; GG – Photograph by Professor Glenn Grieco; LOC – Library
of Congress, Washington, DC; USNHHC – United States Heritage and
History Command. Other sources are listed in full. Kevin Crisman and
Glenn Grieco retain copyright in their illustrations.

Artist's note

Readers may care to note that the original paintings from which the artwork
plates in this book were prepared are available for private sale. All reproduction
copyright whatsoever is retained by the Publishers. All inquiries should be
addressed to:

p.wright1@btinternet.com

The Publishers regret that they can enter into no correspondence upon this matter.

CONTENTS

INTRODUCTION

On the afternoon of September 10, 1813, Master Commandant Oliver Hazard Perry, United States Navy, dashed off two brief notes reporting a victory over the Royal Navy squadron on Lake Erie. It was barely 30 minutes after he had received the surrender of the British flagship, HMS *Detroit*, from Lieutenant George Inglis. Inglis started as *Detroit*'s junior lieutenant. By battle's end, he was in charge. All officers more senior were dead or badly wounded. Perry's counterpart, Commander Robert Heriot Barclay, seriously wounded late in the battle, had been taken to the surgeon.

Perry hastily wrote his two messages aboard the sloop-of-war USS *Niagara*. He had started the battle aboard USS *Lawrence*, a sister ship to *Niagara* but after *Lawrence* was pounded to a wreck, he boarded *Niagara* to continue the fight. His first message, sent to Major General William Henry Harrison commanding United States Army forces in the Northwest United States, was two lines long. It read: "Dear Gen'l: We have met the enemy, and they are ours, two ships, two Brigs one schooner & one sloop. Yours with great respect and esteem. O H Perry." Minutes later, he jotted down a slightly longer message to Secretary of the Navy William Jones:

U.S. Brig *Niagara* off the Western Sister
Head of Lake Erie, Sept. 10th. 1813
4p.m.

It has pleased the Almighty to give to the arms of the United States a signal Victory over their enemies on this Lake – The British squadron consisting of two Ships, two Brigs one Schooner & one Sloop have this moment surrendered to the force under

my command, after a Sharp conflict. I have the honor to be Sir Very Respectfully Your Obdt. Servt.

O.H. Perry

It *was* a signal victory. An entire British squadron, down to its smallest vessel, had surrendered to an enemy naval force after a battle; the only instance in naval history so crushing a victory was achieved over the Royal Navy. Equally remarkable was the battle's location – the western end of freshwater Lake Erie, 500 miles from the Atlantic Ocean. It was to 1813 what a battle on the Moon might be today. It took longer to travel from New York City or Montreal to Put-in-Bay, where the battle was fought, than for the Apollo space missions to fly from the Earth to the Moon.

All vessels involved in the battle had been built on Lake Erie or adjoining rivers and lakes. The timber to build the ships was available locally. Everything else to build and man the ships, except drinking water, had to be transported. Artillery, iron fittings, munitions, clothing, most of the crews, and even most food, painstakingly traveled to Lake Erie via wilderness roads and inland rivers. While wind aided movement on open water, most goods were moved by muscle – oxen or horses pulling wagons, or men paddling bateaux.

Some vessels in the Battle of Lake Erie had been prewar civilian ships, built to haul cargo. These were hastily converted to warships by adding guns. Most had been built as warships, however, the majority knocked together after war was declared in June

Perry boarded HMS *Detroit* to accept the formal surrender of the British ships only minutes before returning to USS *Niagara* to write his dispatches announcing the victory to Major General William Henry Harrison and Secretary of the Navy William Jones. [AC]

The US view of what the reaction to Perry's victory would be in Britain is encapsulated in this cartoon, showing Queen Charlotte offering King George III a bottle of perry – a pun about the US victor's name. (AC)

Queen Charlotte and Johnny Bull got their dose of Perry.

There were numerous skirmishes between sloops-of-war on the Lakes, but most were inconclusive. One such, fought November 8, 1812 on Lake Ontario, involved HMS *Royal George* (20 guns) and USS *Oneida* (18 guns). (USNHHC)

1812. Both sides created a shipbuilding industry on Lake Erie, churning out hulls, then arming and outfitting them.

All the purpose-built warships shared another characteristic. They were the same class of warship: sloops-of-war. A sloop-of-war had one complete gun deck with the crew living in a berth deck below the gun deck. Frigates too had one gun

deck, but they also mounted guns on raised quarterdecks and forecastles. The sloop-of-war, the most common warship commissioned by navies, was smaller still. They were maids-of-all-work. Oceangoing sloops-of-war served as convoy escorts, scouts, pirate hunters, and commerce raiders. On the Lakes, during the War of 1812, the sloop-of-war started off as the standard warship used for command of the waters. On Lake Ontario and Lake Champlain, the sloop-of-war was replaced in the line of battle by larger frigates and even ships-of-the-line; but on remote Lake Erie it proved impractical to build larger warships, and so the sloop-of-war remained dominant.

Made by the ladies of Erie, Pennsylvania, this flag, emblazoned with James Lawrence's dying words – "DONT GIVE UP THE SHIP" – flew from the top of *Lawrence*'s main mast. Following victory, it and the flags captured from the British were sent to Washington, DC. Since 1849 it has been displayed at the United States Naval Academy. (AC)

On the oceans, sloops-of-war often sailed and fought independently. Perry's friend, James Lawrence, commanding the American sloop-of-war USS *Hornet*, captured the British sloop-of-war HMS *Peacock* in a single-ship duel. It was one of several successful single-ship duels between sloops-of-war won by the US Navy. Gaining promotion from master commandant to captain, Lawrence was given the frigate USS *Chesapeake*.

Emboldened by this easy victory over an incompetent British captain, in June 1813 Lawrence foolishly matched the green crew of *Chesapeake* against the finest frigate crew in the Royal Navy, that of HMS *Shannon*. In a 15-minute action Lawrence was mortally wounded. Despite his call of "don't give up the ship," *Chesapeake* was taken. Grief-stricken over his friend's death, Perry named his flagship *Lawrence*, and adopted Lawrence's dying words as a motto. A flag emblazoned "DONT GIVE UP THE SHIP" flew at *Lawrence*'s maintop during the Battle of Lake Erie. Perry's victory avenged Lawrence's death.

Perry's victory was a squadron action, not a single-ship duel. Ironically, despite both Perry's and Barclay's intentions to fight a line-of-battle action, the actual battle devolved into a series of single-ship actions. A second British sloop-of-war, HMS *Queen Charlotte*, took part in the action, as did seven American schooners, and four other small British warships.

The Battle of Lake Erie had greater strategic consequences than all other single-ship duels fought during the War of 1812 put together. Perry's victory ensured the American Northwest Territory with the northwestern corner of the state of Ohio remained undisputedly under the control of the United States for the rest of the war. Had Barclay's force prevailed, part or all this region might have reverted to Britain in a peace negotiated on terms less favorable to the United States. Within a century the states carved from this territory formed the United States' industrial heartland – the Arsenal of Democracy which helped Britain survive two world wars in the 20th century – yet this outcome was decided by a duel between *Lawrence* and *Detroit* followed by a duel between *Niagara* and *Detroit*. Rarely had such a fight between such small ships yielded greater results.

CHRONOLOGY

1785
August 23   Oliver Hazard Perry is born.

1786
September 18   Robert Heriot Barclay is born.

1798
May   Barclay joins the Royal Navy as
               a midshipman.

1799
April 7   Perry joins the US Navy as
               a midshipman.

1805
November 11   Barclay is promoted to lieutenant.

1807
               Perry is promoted to lieutenant.

1810
               Queen Charlotte is launched.

1812
June 18   The War of 1812 starts.
August 16   The British capture Detroit.
October 6   Perry is promoted to
               master commandant.
September   Black Rock is established as a US
               naval base.
October   Daniel Dobbins establishes a
               shipyard at Presque Isle
               (Erie, Pennsylvania).
October 8   US Navy forces commanded by Jesse
               Elliott capture HMS *Detroit*
               (formerly USS *Adams*) and
               HMS *Caledonia*.

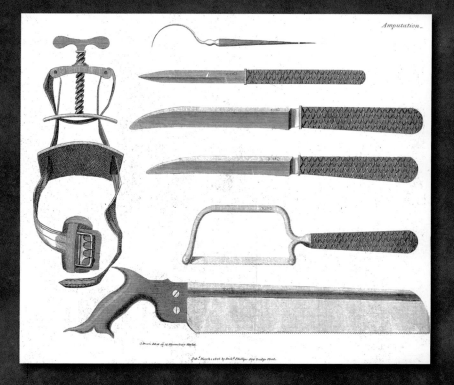

Medical technology of 1813 was brutal and basic, with amputation the treatment for most combat limb injuries. Naval surgeons used tools like these for battle casualties. The illustration comes from *The Naval Surgeon*, a book for Royal Navy surgeons published in 1806. (AC)

1813

February 18	Noah and Adam Brown and 15 carpenters and blacksmiths are sent to Erie, Pennsylvania to build 20-gun brigs *Lawrence* and *Niagara*.
March 27	Perry and 150 sailors arrive at Presque Isle.
May 24	*Lawrence* is launched.
June 4	*Niagara* is launched.
June 5	Barclay and 25 officers and men arrive at Amherstburg, where he takes command of the British squadron on Lake Erie.
June 8	Barclay begins a blockade of the US Navy squadron at Presque Isle.
July 28	Barclay lifts the blockade of Presque Isle.
August	The all-new HMS *Detroit* is launched.
August 1	*Lawrence* and *Niagara* are brought across the sandbar at Presque Isle.
August 9	Elliott arrives at Erie with five small warships and 120 sailors.
August 12	Perry establishes a blockade of Amherstburg.
September 9	Barclay sails to engage the US flotilla.
September 10	The Battle of Lake Erie.
September 26	Perry transports Harrison's army to Canada.
October 5	The Battle of the Thames.
November	Perry is promoted to captain, backdated to September 10.

1814

July	Perry is given command of USS *Java*.

1815

February 17	The Treaty of Ghent is ratified, ending the War of 1812.

1817

April 29	The Rush–Bagot Treaty is signed, demilitarizing the Great Lakes.

1819

August	Perry is placed in command of anti-piracy efforts in the West Indies.
August 23	Perry dies of yellow fever off Venezuela.

Three veterans of the Battle of Lake Erie, *Niagara*, USS *Scorpion*, and USS *Tigress*, managed to trap and destroy the armed sloop HMS *Nancy* during a battle in Georgian Bay on August 14, 1814. *Nancy* was the sole remaining British ship in the Upper Lakes after the Battle of Lake Erie due to its presence on Lake Huron at the time. (USNHHC)

1824

October	Barclay is promoted to captain.

1825

	US Navy sells *Detroit* and *Queen Charlotte*.

1837

May 8	Barclay dies.

1841

September	*Detroit* is sent down the Niagara River to go over the Falls as a spectacle. It runs aground before reaching the Falls.

1844

	Queen Charlotte is scrapped.

1876

	Lawrence, sent to Philadelphia as an exhibit in the Centennial International Exhibition of 1876, is destroyed when the warehouse it is stored in burns.

1913

April	*Niagara* is refloated for display during the Battle of Lake Erie Centennial.

DESIGN AND DEVELOPMENT

At the start of the 19th century, any sailing warship with all of its guns on one deck fell into the category of sloop-of-war. A sloop-of-war carried as few as six guns or as many as 22. A naval ship too small to mount six guns would be considered a dispatch vessel. A naval ship mounting more than 22 guns mounted some on raised quarterdecks or forecastles, in addition to the battery on the gun deck. If it mounted guns on both forecastles and quarterdeck, it was considered a frigate. If it carried guns only on the quarterdeck, it was counted as a post ship in the Royal Navy, or a jackass frigate (or even a frigate) in other navies.

THE SLOOP-OF-WAR

The sloop-of-war was one of the oldest classes of sailing warships, tracing its ancestry to the single-deck race-built galleons of Elizabethan times. *Golden Hind*, 300 tons, with its single gun deck and 22 guns, would have been rated as a sloop-of-war by the Georgian Royal Navy. Yet the sloop-of-war of the early 19th century was significantly different than the earliest generations of single gun deck warships, having evolved as a "frigate-built" vessel. This term described a ship with its guns on the upper deck, and a lower deck primarily given over to crew accommodation. Some sloops-of-war were built to this pattern before the frigate emerged. The frigate, which appeared in the 1740s, popularized this architecture by moving the battery

carried on the lower deck to the upper deck. The lighter battery originally mounted on the upper deck was eliminated.

The sloop-of-war evolved from demi-batterie warships, which appeared in the late 1600s. These vessels were designed to carry a flush battery on the upper deck, with provisions for a few heavy guns on the lower deck, the belief being the heavy guns would provide a light warship with a hefty punch. In practice, the lower deck was so close to the water, especially on the downwind side as the ship heeled, as to be virtually useless. The lower gun ports weakened the hull, and offered entry for water in rough weather. Demi-batterie designs were largely abandoned by the 1720s, although they occasionally appeared through 1750.

While demi-batterie ports were eliminated, ports for sweeps (large oars) remained on the lower deck for the next few decades. Sweeps allowed a small warship to move and maneuver in calm airs. As with gun ports, lower-deck oar ports created a wet ship; and by the American Revolutionary War, these too moved to the upper deck. Whether the lower deck continued to be called the gun deck (despite the absence of guns), the lower deck, or the berth deck, removing its hull openings created drier accommodations and allowed the sleeping quarters to remain warmer in cold weather, all of which yielded healthier crews. It also made preparing for action easier by reducing the number of objects unrelated to combat on the deck carrying the guns – but it did not necessarily reduce the crowding.

A sloop-of-war typically had only two decks. The upper deck was a weather deck, exposed to the elements. Sometimes the after third of the upper deck was sheltered by a raised quarterdeck. That section of the upper deck was used for the captain's cabin. Less frequently, especially toward the end of the 18th century, there would be a raised forecastle, too. After 1800, flush deck sloops-of-war came into fashion, pushing the captain's quarters into the lower deck, displacing the officers' cabins forward, and reducing the space available for the sailors.

The volume below the upper deck offered little relief, it being occupied by the hold used for storage and a series of platforms, known as the orlop. In larger frigates the

The crowded nature of the sloop-of-war is illustrated in this cutaway, drawn by Professor Kevin Crisman, of USS *Jefferson*, a 20-gun sloop-of-war built on Lake Ontario in 1814. Note the crowded living quarters, the placement of stores in odd corners, and the height of the bulwarks, once the hammocks are placed in the nettings on top of the bulwarks. (KC)

depth of hold – the distance between the keel and the lower deck – permitted a second tier of cabins for the lesser officers. A sloop-of-war was too shallow and too small for this. The platforms were crammed with stores needed to operate the ship: the sail locker, the magazine, and various store rooms for items which could not be kept in the hold. Its hold had to carry stores allowing it to remain at sea for as long as the frigate. The sailors were crowded into the forward two-thirds or half of the lower deck. Yet although crowded by the standards of a frigate, the sloop-of-war was less crowded than a ship-of-the-line or two-decker, in which part of the crew had to share sleeping space with the ship's guns. Also, a sloop-of-war carried fewer men than a frigate. A Royal Navy frigate required a crew of 220–280 officers, sailors, and marines. A 20-gun sloop-of-war required only 160, while a ten-gun sloop could be manned by as few as 100.

Sloops-of-war were crowded for another reason. Sailing ships had an optimal length-to-breadth-to-depth ratio. The length of the ship at the waterline was 3.4 to 3.8 times greater than the breadth of the ship. A ship's draft was typically one-seventh to one-eighth of its length at the waterline. The structural limitations of wood yielded the ratio used for the hull dimensions: narrower ships tended to break apart due to wave action working over the length of the ship; wider ships moved too slowly and were hard to steer. Similarly, a ship's draft was dictated by its length. A ship much shallower than one-eighth of its length could be pushed sideways by wind, rendering it uncontrollable in gales. A ship much deeper than one-seventh of its length could not use many seaports.

Smaller ships could and occasionally were built to a much higher length-to-breadth ratio. One class of sloop-of-war popular in the first half of the 18th century was the "galley." Primarily a sailing vessel, its narrow hull form allowed it to be rowed in light winds. These ships had a length-to-breadth ratio from 4.5 to 5.2. However, the narrow hull limited the amount of stores these ships could carry and tended to wear out faster than conventional counterparts. By 1790 they had largely fallen out of use.

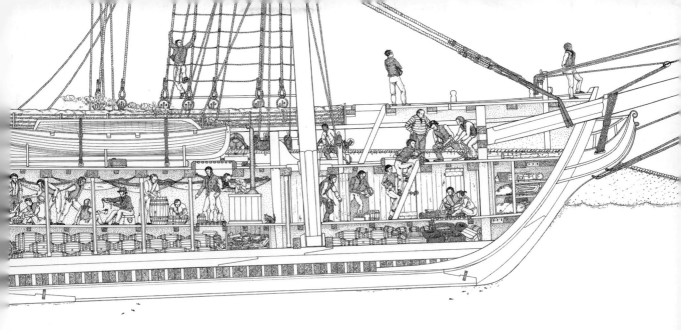

Sloops-of-war were small ships, typically 60–110ft long. Their draft ranged between 8ft and 15ft, and even the largest sloop-of-war could not place the lower deck more than 5–6ft below the upper deck. Deck beams further limited headroom. A man of average height for the time, 5ft 8in, had to walk stooped on the lower deck.

Sloop-of-war armament also evolved over the life of the class. From their emergence and from the 1690s through the 1780s, sloops-of-war carried a battery of 4-pdr or 6-pdr smoothbore muzzle-loading long guns. Even into the 1790s many sloops-of-war were so armed. In 1801, Lord Cochrane, commanding the 14-gun sloop-of-war HMS *Speedy*, boasted he could carry a broadside in his coat. With *Speedy*'s 4-pdr guns, a seven-gun broadside weighed but 28lb.

The late 1770s saw the introduction of a new type of gun, the carronade. Short-barreled and short-range, a carronade weighed as much as a long gun throwing a ball one-quarter the weight of the carronade's shot. A ship built to carry 4-pdr long guns could comfortably mount 18-pdr carronades, while a ship designed for 6-pdr long guns could replace them with 24-pdr carronades. The transition from long guns to carronades took place in the 1790s, and by 1801 *Speedy*'s 4-pdr battery was anachronistic.

Both the United States Navy and Royal Navy enthusiastically rearmed their sloops-of-war with carronades. By 1810 a 20-gun sloop-of-war typically carried nothing but 32-pdr carronades (except for two long guns in the bows, used as chase guns) and could fire 300lb of iron with every broadside. The standard 36-gun frigate of 1770 had a broadside weight of 186lb, one-third smaller. Given the light scantlings of the sloop-of-war, these ships were eggshells armed with hammers.

One thing not uniform about a sloop-of-war was its rig. Larger warships were almost inevitably ship-rigged. They carried three masts – fore, main, and mizzen – with square sails on all three masts. Some sloops-of-war were also ship-rigged, especially the larger ones, sometimes called ship-sloops. Less common in 1812, but used more frequently after the war ended, were barque rigs. With barques, the after mast had no square sails, hung from spars running athwart the ship. The mizzen had

HMS *Wolfe* was a typical oceangoing Royal Navy sloop-of-war. Brig-rigged, and armed with 18 guns, it provided a naval presence strong enough to discourage pirates or privateers at an economical cost. *Wolfe* is shown hove-to, stationary while waiting for a pilot boat to lead it into harbor. (AC)

only fore-and-aft sails, these being triangular and trapezoidal sails running the length of the ship. The sloop-of-war HMS *Beagle*, based on a Napoleonic design for a brig-sloop, was rigged as a barque prior to its voyage with Charles Darwin in 1831–36.

Other sloops-of-war carried two masts, with virtually every rig used on two-masted sailing ships. Brig rigs – two masts carrying square sails, with the larger main mast aft of the smaller, or fore mast – were the most common. A variant of this was the "snow," virtually indistinguishable from a brig at a distance. It carried a short mast immediately aft of the main mast on which the boom and gaff holding the trapezoidal spanker sail was set. Both were called brig-sloops.

Some sloops-of-war were ketch-rigged, with the forward mast being the main mast and larger than the after mizzen mast. While popular imagination assigns all ketch-rigged warships as mortar-carrying bomb ketches, in reality many ketches were standard cruising warships, while many bomb vessels were ship-rigged. USS *Intrepid*, used to burn USS *Philadelphia* in Tripoli Harbor in February 1804, was a ketch.

Some two-masted sloops-of-war were also schooner-rigged, with fore-and-aft sails on both masts, but carrying square topsails and topgallant sails. USS *Enterprise*, the "Lucky Little *Enterprise*" of Barbary War and War of 1812 fame, started as a schooner. These vessels would be called schooner-sloops.

About the only rig never used on a sloop-of-war was a sloop rig: a single-masted ship with fore-and-aft sails. While common with dispatch vessels, a single mast made it difficult to turn a vessel quickly. A sloop rig worked well on a dispatch vessel which was intended to carry messages swiftly, and which was not expected to fight other warships.

Rigs did not stay constant, however. A sloop-of-war could start off with one rig and be converted to another. *Enterprise*, for example, was re-rigged as a brig prior to the War of 1812. *Beagle*, initially intended as a two-masted brig, sailed as a three-masted

barque. The Royal Navy brig-sloops of the Cruizer class and ship-sloops of the Snake class had an identical hull design and both carried 20 guns, but whether the hull became a brig-sloop or a ship-sloop depended on whether it was rigged with two or three masts.

Maneuverability was greater with a three-masted rig than a two-masted rig, but required a greater crew. Fore-and-aft rigs ships required fewer men than square-rigged ships and could sail closer to the wind, but they lacked the ability to stop or turn as quickly. Ketch rigs were less handy than brig rigs. Square-rigged ships had more prestige than fore-and-aft rigs ships, and three-masted vessels were more prestigious than their two-masted counterparts. Navies used a mix of rigs based on manpower pools, perceived needs, and officers' preferences.

Navies used sloops-of-war in many roles. They were equally handy at protecting and destroying commerce, and served as escorts or as commerce raiders depending upon need. Privateers were civilian-owned sloops-of-war, which profited by capturing merchant ships. Naval sloops-of-war escorting a merchant convoy discouraged privateers from attacking because there was no profit in fighting warships. The naval sloop-of-war was strong enough to fight (and usually capture) privateers. Sloops-of-war served as scouts for a fleet of ships-of-the-line, and were valuable in blockade duty. With their shallow draft they could sail closer inshore than bigger ships; and in the absence of larger warships, they could command the seas. Frigates could do everything

Launched in 1813, USS *Erie* was typical of the oceangoing ship-sloops built by the US Navy during the War of 1812. Trapped by the British blockade of Hampton Roads, its crew was transferred as a body to USS *Jefferson*, a similar-sized sloop-of-war on Lake Ontario. (NARA)

a sloop-of-war could do, and generally do it better, but they also required a much greater commitment of resource. For the cost of four 38-gun frigates a navy could field seven 20-gun or a dozen ten-gun sloops-of-war. Navies needing to cover many different obligations simultaneously often found sloops-of-war invaluable supplements to the larger frigate.

LAKES WARSHIPS

The Saint Lawrence watershed, which includes the Great Lakes and Lake Champlain, contains some of the world's largest bodies of fresh water. By oceanic standards the Great Lakes are small, with a combined surface area of 94,250 square miles. By contrast, the Baltic Sea covers 160,335 square miles and the Black Sea 158,496 square miles.

The largest warship to sail the Great Lakes, HMS *St. Lawrence* was a three-deck ship-of-the-line launched on Lake Ontario in 1814. It mounted 104 guns: 34 32-pdr long guns, 34 24-pdr long guns, 34 32-pdr carronades, and two 68-pdr carronades. (AC)

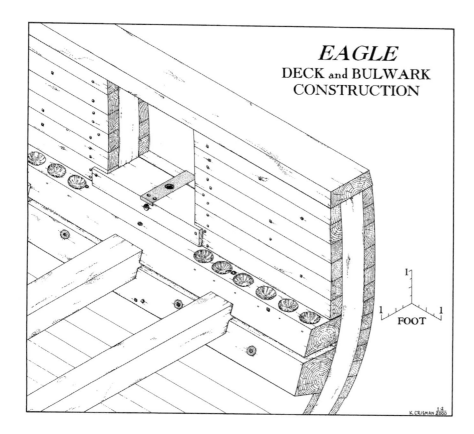

EAGLE DECK and BULWARK CONSTRUCTION

K. CRISMAN 2000

FOOT

Because of a lack of adequate curved timber and in an effort to reduce construction time, most Lakes warships were built without knees. Instead, as shown in this drawing by Professor Kevin Crisman, clamps – long, thick beams which ran along the length of the ship – supported the deck beams. (KC)

Small does not mean insignificant, however. The English Channel, one of the world's most strategically important bodies of water, is 28,985 square miles, smaller than Lake Superior's 31,700 square miles. Shallow Lake Erie – surface area 7,410 square miles and average depth of 62ft – and small Lake Ontario – surface area 7,340 square miles and average depth of 283ft – were large enough for oceangoing ships. By the end of the War of 1812 Lake Ontario had five ships-of-the-line afloat or under construction, all of which were bigger than HMS *Victory*.

Lakes vessels may have been as large and as powerful as their oceangoing counterparts, but they were different in several ways. The Lakes are freshwater bodies. A cubic foot of salt water weighs 64lb whereas a cubic foot of fresh water weighs 62¼lb, so a Lakes ship had to displace 3 percent more volume for the same tonnage as an oceangoing ship. A larger percentage of the area of a lake was shoal water when compared to an ocean or sea, so a ship designed to operate on the Lakes had to be built to draw less water than a similar vessel intended for the ocean. This combination made Lakes ships more subject to the effect of wind, with wind from abeam more likely to push a Lakes ship sideways than it could its deeper-keeled equivalent moving through denser seawater.

Fresh water freezes more readily than salt water. Except for the Arctic regions, most oceanic bodies remain largely ice-free during winters. With the exception of the Baltic Sea (where ice constrained movement between November and March) and the occasional frozen-in northern European port, naval activity at the time was a year-round affair on the oceans. On the Lakes, however, November marked a period of pause until the thaws came in March or April.

Freshwater navigation offered compensations. The *Teredo navalis*, or shipworm, was a clam which tunneled through wood and could reduce an unprotected hull to a leaking sponge of tunnels. The shipworm was a saltwater creature, which died in fresh water, so Lakes vessels could forgo the copper sheathing used by navies since the 1770s to protect the hulls of their oceangoing ships.

The small size of the Lakes limited wave activity. Even on shallow Lake Erie, notorious for lake storms that could whip up waves higher than those of its sister lakes, those waves could not match the stresses on a hull created by a North Atlantic winter storm or the towering rollers kicked up by Roaring Forties in the southern hemisphere. A Lakes ship therefore required lighter scantlings than a ship built for the oceans.

These factors yielded lightly built ships with saucer-shaped cross-sections. They could be built with a minimum of metal fittings. Copper sheathing was unnecessary, and wooden pegs – treenails (pronounced "trunnels") – could substitute for iron nails for most purposes. Some iron fittings were needed, but no more than could be carried by a wagon.

While a Lakes warship's shallow hull reduced its depth of hold, it did not need the storage capacity of an oceangoing vessel. Even the smaller crews of a sloop-of-war required large quantities of drinking water to remain at sea, so a sloop-of-war making a transatlantic crossing filled much of the volume of its hold with casks of water – at least enough to quench the thirst of its crew for a month. A Lakes sloop-of-war could renew its water with a bucket dropped over the side, so a few days' supply was all it needed.

Food was a similar story. While a ship crossing an ocean might not see land for weeks, or even months, a vessel on the Great Lakes could reach a coast within a day. With the exception of a need to blockade an enemy port, carrying a week's worth of food would meet most operational needs. A blockade could be maintained so long as there were a few vessels available to carry supplies between a friendly port and the blockading squadron.

The chief challenge the shallow hull presented a naval ship was finding a safe place for the magazine, which was supposed to be below the waterline. A Lakes sloop-of-war typically drew less than 12ft. Part of the lowest part of the hold had to be used for ballast because a naval warship's tall masts created a lot of torque for winds to heel the ship, which had to be counteracted by ballast. It was therefore difficult to place the magazine without the upper part intruding on the already-crowded lower deck.

Oceangoing and Lakes sloops both had a sizable battery of guns – both British and American navies shared a love of the biggest possible weight of broadside – so a Lakes sloop-of-war needed a roomy magazine. A 20-gun sloop with a battery of 32-pdr carronades burned almost 25lb of gunpowder – the content of one powder keg – with each broadside fired, and Royal Navy and US Navy captains of the War of 1812 held to a standard of three broadsides every two minutes. Firing at this rate for 20 minutes consumed 750lb of gunpowder.

The Lakes sloop-of-war was a vessel which was crowded, powerfully armed for its size, and slightly less handy than its oceangoing counterpart. It required careful handling because it was "tender" – the high center of gravity due to its shallow hull and lofty mast meant it could capsize more easily than an oceangoing vessel – but properly handled it could sail swiftly and hit hard.

AMERICAN CONSTRUCTION

The United States had a naval presence on the various lakes of the St. Lawrence watershed over a shorter period than the British, due in part to its shorter existence as a nation. It had not declared independence until 1776, and had not received British recognition of its independence until 1783, with the signing of the Treaty of Ghent. While a Continental fleet had been built on Lake Champlain in 1776, it was destroyed by the Royal Navy that year. Thereafter, until peace was signed, Britain dominated the Lakes.

Even after the peace, the US Navy made a tardy arrival on the Lakes. The British occupied much of the Old Northwest Territory, parts of modern Michigan, Indiana, Illinois, and Wisconsin, until the signing of the Jay Treaty in 1795. This effectively denied naval access to Lake Huron, Lake Michigan, and Lake Superior. New York and Pennsylvania bordered Lake Champlain, Lake Ontario, and Lake Erie, but even there a United States presence was limited. The new nation did not create the Revenue-Marine (today's United States Coast Guard) until 1790. The Continental Navy was disbanded in 1784, and not reestablished as the US Navy until the Naval Act of 1794. Neither service maintained vessels on the Lakes until after 1800.

This did not mean there was no shipbuilding on the Lakes by the United States. By the 1790s the Lakes were commercial arteries, and shipyards dotted the lake shores of New York and Pennsylvania. They were surrounded by abundant sources of timber. Their products were largely schooner-rigged or brig-rigged vessels, typically less than 100ft in length. As with other commercial sailing ships of the era, these vessels could be armed and used as warships. During the War of 1812 both sides purchased around two-dozen schooners and brigs between them, arming them as either sloops-of-war or gunboats (carrying one large gun, typically on a pivot).

The United States did not establish naval yards or bases until after commissioning its first warship on the Lakes in 1809. That vessel, the brig-rigged *Oneida*, of 18 guns, was built at a commercial yard in Oswego, New York, on Lake Ontario. It was constructed by Henry Eckford, a shipbuilder who previously built gunboats for the US Navy at his Long Island, New York shipyard. With an actual ship on Lake Ontario, the US Navy set up a base at Sacketts Harbor, in an anchorage protected by a small fort.

Once the War of 1812 commenced, the US Navy was forced to make up for lost time. Sacketts Harbor was heavily fortified and the US Navy established a

Daniel Dobbins, a Pennsylvania shipbuilder, shipowner, and ship captain, convinced the Navy Department that Erie, Pennsylvania was the best place to locate a shipyard on Lake Erie. He superintended the construction of four schooners there, and commanded USS *Ohio* as a master. (AC)

major shipyard there, which eventually built five sloops-of-war, two frigates, and two ships-of-the-line. On Lake Champlain it set up operations at Vergennes, Vermont where three sloops-of-war were constructed.

Lake Erie offered a challenge, as the two commercial shipyards which could have proved useful were unavailable. Detroit, in the Michigan Territory, was captured by the British shortly after the war's opening. Black Rock, New York, on the Niagara River, was too threatened by British forces in Canada across the Niagara River. Instead, a shipyard was established at Presque Isle, across a small harbor from Erie, Pennsylvania. Work building the yard began in November 1812. By March 1813 six ships were approaching completion.

The sloops-of-war built on the Lakes were virtually all the largest examples of their class when constructed, but two schooner-rigged vessels represented the smaller class of sloop-of-war. The rest carried 16–26 guns. All the carronades were at least 32-pdrs and most of the long guns fired 12–24lb shot. In many ways they were miniature frigates. The two brigs built on Lake Erie had broadsides almost 50 percent heavier than the broadside of the Continental Navy's USS *Hancock*, a 32-gun frigate.

The US Navy modified the designs of oceangoing sloops-of-war for their Lakes vessels. USS *Jefferson* and USS *Jones*, built late in the war on Lake Ontario, were copies of the Peacock-class sloops-of-war the US Navy was having built for ocean service. Noah and Adam Brown, who built *Lawrence* and *Niagara*, were already well known for the privateers they designed and built in 1812, most notably *General Armstrong* and *Prince de Neufchatel*. The Lakes sloops-of-war may have been built far from the ocean, but they represented cutting-edge shipbuilding.

USS *LAWRENCE*

Length between perpendiculars: 110ft
Breadth: 30ft
Depth of hold: 9ft
Draft: 10ft 6in
Displacement: 493 tons
Armament at battle: 18 32-pdr carronades, two 12-pdr long guns. Total weight of broadside: 300lb
Crew (at battle): 134
Laid down: March 1813, Presque Isle (Erie), Pennsylvania
Launched: May 24, 1813
Commissioned: August 4, 1813

Laid down, built, and launched in less than 90 days, *Lawrence* was one of two 20-gun sloops-of-war designed and built by Noah and Adam Brown at Presque Isle, Pennsylvania. Once commissioned it gave the United States Navy command of Lake Erie. *Lawrence* served as Master Commander Oliver Hazard Perry's flagship at the Battle of Lake Erie on September 10, 1813. Fighting virtually the entire British fleet on its own, *Lawrence* was forced to surrender after a long fight but was recaptured when Perry brought *Niagara* into action.

Lawrence served with the US Navy fleet on Lake Huron and Lake Erie in 1814, including an unsuccessful attempt to recapture Mackinaw Island. After the end of the war, in 1815, *Lawrence* was submerged in Misery Bay (next to Presque Isle) for preservation. The submerged hull was sold in 1825. It was raised briefly for examination in 1836, then resubmerged. In September 1875 *Lawrence* was raised, cut into pieces, and transported to Philadelphia, Pennsylvania. There the hull was reassembled for display at the 1876 Centennial of the United States Exhibition. Before the Exhibition started, however, the warehouse in which the ship was stored caught fire, and *Lawrence* destroyed.

Amherstburg, located on the Detroit River just above where its mouth entered Lake Erie, was the main naval base for Provincial Marine and Royal Navy forces on the Upper Lakes. In 1812 it also had the only shipyard available to the British that was capable of building warships. (AC)

BRITISH CONSTRUCTION

Britain had built sloops-of-war on the Great Lakes and St. Lawrence watershed (including Lake Champlain) since the 1750s. In 1756, during the French and Indian War, a 16-gun snow-rigged sloop-of-war was built at Oswego. The ship, HMS *Halifax*, carried 16 6-pdr guns – a formidable armament even for an oceangoing sloop-of-war of the day.

By 1812 Britain had two shipyards each on Lake Ontario and Lake Erie. On Lake Ontario it had the Kingston Royal Navy Dockyard (today the site of the Royal Military College of Canada) and Naval Shipyard, York at York (today Toronto), Ontario. On Lake Erie were the Navy Island Royal Naval Shipyard at Navy Island on the Niagara River and the Amherstburg Royal Naval Dockyard on the Detroit River. The British government purchased land for a shipyard on Lake Huron which became the Penetanguishene Naval Yard in 1813 and planned a naval depot at the mouth of Grand River; where Maitland, Ontario is today. To cover Lake Champlain, it built warships at Fort St. Jean on the Richelieu River during the American Revolutionary War, and established a yard on Ile aux Noix in 1813.

Between 1764, when Britain acquired Canada from France, and 1776, when the United States declared independence, British government vessels provided maritime security, enforcing laws and maintaining peace. Sloops-of-war filled those functions admirably. During the American Revolutionary War Britain built several sloops-of-war on all of the Lakes, including ten large ones capable of mounting 16–26 guns. Since there was then little commercial traffic on the Lakes, all were built as warships.

Once the Treaty of Paris was signed in 1783 and American independence recognized, the Lakes' status changed from an internal waterway to part of a national frontier. Over the next decade Britain's Lakes warships continued to provide maritime security and transportation for the government. Increasingly, however, they were also intended to provide a naval presence if war with the United States ever erupted. Immediately following American independence, Britain used ships built during the American Revolutionary War. The life of a ship in government service on the Lakes averaged ten years, and by the 1790s new sloops-of-war were being built to replace

HMS *DETROIT*

Length between perpendiculars: 92ft 6in
Breadth: 26ft
Depth of hold: 11ft
Draft: 12ft
Displacement: 320 tons
Armament at battle: One 18-pdr long gun (on swivel), two 24-pdr long guns, six 12-pdr long guns, eight 9-pdr long guns, one 24-pdr carronade, one 18-pdr carronade. Total weight of broadside: 138lb
Crew (at battle): 150
Laid down: January 1813
Launched: July 1813, Amherstburg, Ontario
Commissioned: August 1813

Built at the Amherstburg Royal Naval Dockyard on the Detroit River, *Detroit* repeated the design of *Queen Charlotte* (also built at Amherstburg) and *Royal George*. Construction progressed slowly due to a shortage of skilled shipwrights

and supplies. It was intended to be armed with four 12-pdr long guns and 16 32-pdr carronades, but the guns were captured by the United States at York, Ontario on April 27, 1813. When completed it was armed with whatever was available, including guns taken from Fort Malden, guarding Amherstburg.

Detroit served as Commander Robert Heriot Barclay's flagship at the Battle of Lake Erie, where it was captured by Perry's fleet. Taken to Put-in-Bay, it wintered there 1813–14. In 1814 *Detroit* was taken to Erie, and served as a receiving ship for the rest of the war. Submerged for preservation in Misery Bay off Presque Isle at war's end, *Detroit* was raised in the 1830s and sold for commercial service. A derelict at Buffalo, New York by 1841, *Detroit* was purchased in September of that year and re-rigged. It was launched down the Niagara River with the intention of creating a spectacle by sailing over Niagara Falls. Instead, the ship grounded on a shoal, and eventually fell to pieces.

Based on the Snake/Cruizer classes of sloops-of-war, *Royal George* was a near-sister to *Queen Charlotte* and *Detroit*. Adaptations made for Lakes service included omission of the quarter galleries its oceangoing counterparts had. *Royal George* was built on Lake Ontario. (KC)

war veterans. Some Lake Erie vessels were built at Detroit, which was not turned over to the United States until after the Jay Treaty was signed in 1795.

Between 1784 and 1805 these ships were effectively a reserve navy; most were manned by skeleton crews and were little more than armed transports. Most British ships built prior to 1807 were small sloops-of-war, under 100 tons, with snow, brig, or schooner rigs. Once war with France resumed in 1803, however, relations between the United States and Britain began to sour. Tensions rose over trade embargos and impressment. In 1805 HMS *Earl of Moira* was launched on Lake Ontario. Originally intended as a small brig, it was ship-rigged and increased to 169 tons. HMS *General Hunter*, launched at Amherstburg in 1807, was only 93 tons and brig-rigged. Intended to replace a ship wrecked in 1805, it was built to the wrecked vessel's plan.

The next two ships built were significantly different. They were Lakes adaptations of the Royal Navy's Snake class, at that time the Royal Navy's largest and most powerful class of ship-sloops. The Snake-class vessels were flush-decked, 100ft long and 30ft across, and normally carried 16 32-pdr carronades and two long guns as bow-chasers.

The Lakes adaptations of these sloops-of-war were slightly smaller, being 4–7ft shorter and 2–4ft narrower. They retained the flush deck, with a shallower draft than their oceangoing counterparts. They also retained the lofty rig of the Snake class, and represented the most powerful warships then on Lake Ontario and Lake Erie. The Lake Ontario vessel was christened *Royal George* when launched in 1809; the Lake Erie vessel, *Queen Charlotte* in 1810. Both were given carronade armament – *Royal George* was outfitted with 32-pdrs; *Queen Charlotte* had 24-pdrs – and were models for the future sloops-of-war built by Britain on the Lakes, especially Lake Ontario and Lake Champlain. Their broadsides grew ever heavier; some mounted 68-pdr carronades, rarely seen on oceangoing warships. On Lake Erie, due to the difficulty of getting guns to the shipyards, no gun or cannon over 24-pdr caliber was mounted on a sloop-of-war.

Over the next five years Britain built 13 more warships on the Lakes. Six were sloops-of-war; the others were frigates and ships-of-the-line. On Lake Erie, sloops-of-war were the largest ships constructed, and the sloop-of-war remained the master of the lake.

THE STRATEGIC SITUATION

The War of 1812 was triggered by impressment and blockade. Britain was conscripting sailors to man the Royal Navy (a process known as impressment) and blockading Continental ports to prevent merchant vessels from trading with France and its allies. Britain justified its actions as necessities in its war with Napoleonic France, a struggle for Britain's very existence.

The United States, the largest seafaring neutral, felt the effects. It resented the interference with its trade the blockade imposed, and was angered by the Royal Navy seizing American sailors for service on British warships. Only British subjects were liable to impressment, but exactly who was "British" was frequently ambiguous. The United States and Britain shared a common language, and some British-born mariners moved to the United States and claimed American citizenship. It was also the case that American-born sailors frequently volunteered for service in the Royal Navy during its wars with France. Throw in an American belief that Britain was supporting indigenous resistance to the United States, and conditions were ripe for conflict.

The result was a war Britain, preoccupied with its struggle with France, did not want. To placate the United States, Britain rescinded the Orders in Council restricting trade two days before the United States declared war. Unfortunately, this failed to have the desired effect of preventing or ending a war with the United States.

Perhaps rescinding the Orders in Council could have defused tensions if the United States had not wanted Canada – a desire which provided the tinder to fuel the sparks created by impressment and blockade into a war over "Free Trade and Sailors' Rights."

Impressment – the conscription of sailors from civilian ships at sea by the Royal Navy – was limited by law to British subjects. Yet Royal Navy warships often stopped US merchant vessels and seized mariners viewed as British regardless of whether they claimed US citizenship. (AC)

In 1812 Canada was still viewed as the 14th colony – the one which failed to achieve independence from Britain. The possibility Francophone and Catholic Quebec might not wish to be part of an English-speaking and largely Protestant United States was ignored. Even if Quebec proved unwilling, modern Ontario (then Upper Canada) was largely unoccupied, offering opportunity for settlers from the Western and New England states. In 1812, many inhabitants of Upper Canada already were United States citizens who had drifted into the open land of the Ontario peninsula.

If the United States ever were to take Canada, 1812 offered the best opportunity. Britain was locked in an apparently losing struggle with France, which, at the zenith of its power, occupied most of Continental Europe and was preparing to invade Russia to force it to submit to French will. Britain had few resources in Upper Canada: two sloops-of-war (the 18-gun *Queen Charlotte* and ten-gun *General Hunter*), two lightly armed schooners of the Provincial Marine (a seagoing militia on the Lakes), several hundred British Army regulars, and perhaps 1,000 local militia. The militia was scattered; assembling more than 400 at one battle was nearly impossible. The British could also call on indigenous allies from the Indian Nations occupying the Old Northwest Territory; but they were undisciplined, hard to control, and the best of their fighters had been killed at the Battle of Tippecanoe in 1811.

The United States could muster nearly 10,000 United States Army regulars and 35,000 militia volunteers raised by the states. These strengths were more theoretical than actual, for the US Army regulars were scattered throughout the United States in small garrisons. On the ends of Lake Erie, the natural invasion routes for Upper Canada, the United States could field a few thousand men at each place. Nor did the United States have naval forces to match even the limited resources of the Provincial Marine. It had but one warship on Lake Erie, the brig USS *Adams* armed with six 6-pdr guns.

To compound the difficulties of both combatants, while Upper Canada promised to be the war's decisive theater it was difficult for either side to reinforce. The Upper Lakes (Erie, Huron, and Michigan) were connected by navigable waterways. Choke points existed at the St. Clair and Detroit rivers (connecting Lake Erie and Lake Huron) and the Straits of Mackinac (separating Lake Huron and Lake Michigan), but a vessel could sail from Black Rock, New York (near Buffalo) to Fort Dearborn (modern Chicago) at the bottom of Lake Michigan. The problem was getting cargo to Lake Erie. Lake Erie and Lake Ontario were separated by the 167ft drop of Niagara Falls.

For the British in Canada the solution lay in a 20-mile portage across the land separating Lake Erie and Lake Ontario. If they controlled Lake Erie they could then sail to their base at Amherstburg on the west end of the lake. If the United States gained mastery of Lake Erie, however, suppliers would have to use a round-about route up the Ottawa River, then portage through wilderness to Lake Nipissing which emptied into Georgian Bay on Lake Huron. Alternatively, they could move overland on unimproved roads through wilderness from Fort York to Amherstburg. Men could march overland, but moving supplies by wagon was fruitless.

There still remained the challenge of getting goods to Lake Ontario. While Quebec could be reached by sea, men and goods had to be transferred to boats which could navigate the upper St. Lawrence River – but rapids and rocks between Montreal and Lake Ontario limited tonnage.

American logistics challenges were even more daunting than those of the British. In short, there were no water routes that did not involve long overland travel. It was 150 miles from Pittsburgh to Erie, the main United States naval base on Lake Erie, and using the Allegheny River required traveling 50 miles by road. Black Rock, on the

Detroit was just a small frontier town in 1812 but its fort, shipyard, and strategic location made it one of the keys to possession of the Michigan Territory. It was one of the last places Britain abandoned after the American Revolutionary War and one of the first occupied after the War of 1812 began. (AC)

Niagara River in New York, was the other naval base on Lake Erie. Part of the journey from New York City to Black Rock could be made via the Hudson and Mohawk rivers, but the rest was overland.

For both sides supply was seasonal: lakes and rivers froze in the winter months, making them unusable. Roads covered with deep snow were passable with sledges, but the cold meant heavy going. Campaigning froze along with the lakes. These difficulties meant few resources would be available to those men on Lake Erie except those already there or what little could be brought in. Men would have to live off the land or go short. In some ways this favored the United States. It had more manpower within marching distance of Upper Canada, and its immediate territory produced more food than Upper Canada. Control of the Lakes meant available supplies could be distributed effectively; but control was more critical for Britain.

In 1812 a combination of British initiative and United States incompetence gave Britain control of the Upper Lakes when, within days of war being declared, British Major-General Sir Isaac Brock sent a force to capture Fort Michilimackinac in the Straits of Mackinac. The United States garrison, unaware of a state of war, was taken by surprise and forced to surrender. Two armed American schooners were captured and added to the Provincial Marine. The British action cut off Lake Michigan, leaving the American force at Fort Dearborn isolated.

Thing went from bad to worse when Brigadier General William Hull invaded Canada July 12. Hull bungled the invasion, alienating the local populace through ill-advised intimidation and the conduct of ill-disciplined American militiamen. Taking counsel of his fears, he then retreated to Detroit where he surrendered his 2,000-man army to a much smaller British force on August 16. In addition to ceding the Michigan Territory, Hull also allowed *Adams*, the only US warship on the Upper Lakes, to fall into British hands. Recommissioned as *Detroit*, it was added to the Provincial Marine.

American fortunes faltered the rest of 1812. The British too suffered a few reverses. On October 8, a boat expedition commanded by the US Navy's Lieutenant Jesse Elliott cut out the brigs *Caledonia* (one of the ships used to capture Fort Michilimackinac) and *Detroit* (formerly *Adams*). *Detroit* was destroyed to prevent

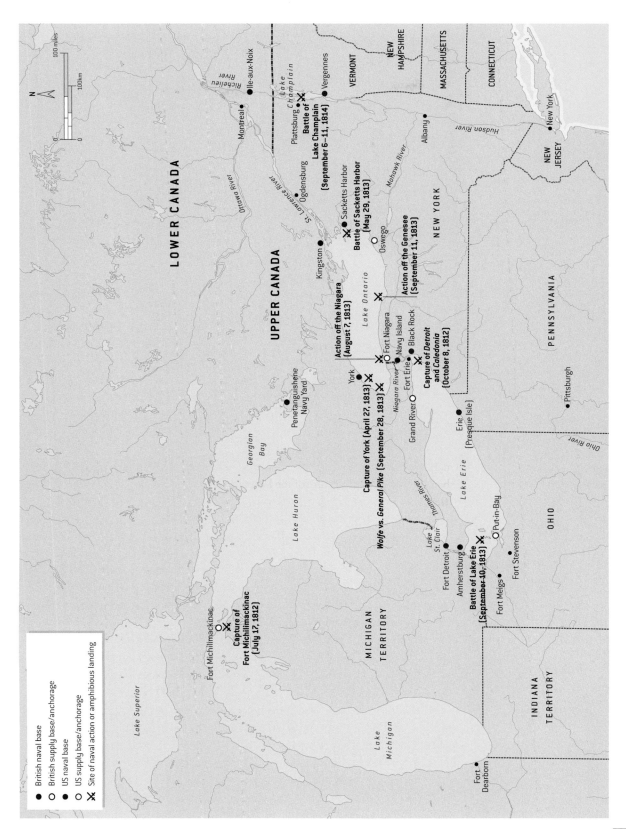

LOWER CANADA

UPPER CANADA

NEW HAMPSHIRE

MASSACHUSETTS

CONNECTICUT

VERMONT

NEW YORK

NEW JERSEY

PENNSYLVANIA

OHIO

INDIANA TERRITORY

MICHIGAN TERRITORY

New York

Albany

Hudson River

Pittsburgh

Ohio River

Mohawk River

Oswego

Sacketts Harbor

Ogdensburg

Montreal

Kingston

York

Penetanguishene Navy Yard

Georgian Bay

Lake Huron

Lake Superior

Lake Michigan

Lake Erie

Lake St. Clair

Fort Detroit

Amherstburg

Thames River

Fort Meigs

Fort Stevenson

Put-in-Bay

Erie (Presque Isle)

Grand River

Fort Erie

Navy Island

Black Rock

Fort Niagara

Niagara River

St. Lawrence River

Ottawa River

Richelieu River

Ile-aux-Noix

Plattsburg

Vergennes

Lake Champlain

Lake Ontario

Fort Michilimackinac

Fort Dearborn

Capture of Fort Michilimackinac (July 17, 1812)

Battle of Lake Erie (September 10, 1813)

Wolfe vs. General Pike (September 28, 1813)

Capture of York (April 27, 1813)

Action off the Niagara (August 7, 1813)

Capture of Detroit and Caledonia (October 8, 1812)

Action of the Genesee (September 11, 1813)

Battle of Sacketts Harbor (May 29, 1813)

Battle of Lake Champlain (September 6–11, 1814)

N

100 miles

100km

- British naval base
- ○ British supply base/anchorage
- ● US naval base
- ○ US supply base/anchorage
- ✕ Site of naval action or amphibious landing

The United States faced an even more formidable logistics challenge on Lake Erie than did the British. An example was the supply of Perry's ships with the necessary gunpowder, which had to be moved from the Dupont mill in Philadelphia to Erie by powder wagons, as shown here. (LOC)

recapture, but *Caledonia* made it to Black Rock, where it was added to the US Navy. Three civilian schooners also at Black Rock were purchased and armed, creating a small four-ship squadron.

As 1812 drew to a close, the United States took additional steps to regain control of Lake Erie. In late fall a shipyard was established across the harbor from Erie, Pennsylvania. Four gunboats were ordered built there, but the order was later modified with the addition of two 300-ton brigs to the construction list. A master commandant (a rank equivalent to the Royal Navy's commander), Oliver Hazard Perry, was sent to command the new squadron emerging in the Pennsylvania wilderness, along with a force of sailors and marines. The US government was determined that 1813 would have a different outcome.

Meanwhile, across the lake, British concerns about the resurgent US Navy were growing. The British built an additional sloop-of-war in 1812, a 13-gun schooner named HMS *Lady Prevost*, but were worried about the reported US Navy brig-sloops being built at Erie. Dependent upon food purchased from Ohio farmers, the British understood that maintaining control of Lake Erie was critical. With this in mind they began building another ship-rigged sloop-of-war, a near-sister to *Queen Charlotte* at Amherstburg. It would be christened *Detroit*.

TECHNICAL SPECIFICATIONS

THE HULL

Lakes sloops-of-war, especially those built during the War of 1812, were of different construction to oceangoing sloops-of-war. Not only did the hull shape differ, but the way in which the hull was built was significantly different. This was due in part to available resources. Between 1790 and 1830 the Lakes were frontier territory in which no extensive ironworks to supply fittings, ropewalks for cordage or mills for sailcloth existed. Timber was abundant, but seasoned timber – dried to remove sap – was scarce. The old-growth forests of the Great Lakes Basin had massive oaks, but they were straight, without the spreading branches seen on lone trees. Compass timber – curved wood used for the bow and stern, and the "L"-shaped knees used to attach the deck to the sides – was difficult to find.

Even during peacetime, Lakes shipwrights worked around problems arising from limited compass timber. The Lakes ships tended to be finer than their seagoing counterparts. Instead of an almost hemispherical bow common on the oceangoing warships of the day, the bows tended to be narrower, presaging the Baltimore clipper of a decade or two later. This feature reduced the curvature needed in the wood. Shipwrights could use heavier frames if desired. One trick frequently used was limiting the number of curved pieces by scarfing together straight timbers to create a curve. Even small ships often had ribs built by scarfing together five pieces of timber where the same-size saltwater ship might only use two pieces. Straight timber was also frequently curved by heating and steaming.

A model of a Lakes sloop-of-war built by Professor Glenn Grieco of Texas A&M University's Ship Model Laboratory reveals the straightforward techniques used – few curved timbers, an absence of knees, and heavy frames. The short mast behind the main mast in this brig-sloop is the snow mast, used for the spanker sail. *Lawrence* and *Niagara* were snows. (GG)

One technique to reduce compass timber use involved eliminating the use of knees. To achieve this, a heavy beam running the length of the ship would be attached to the ribs below the level of the deck beams. The deck beams were then placed on top of this clamp. For added strength a second beam was attached above the deck beams. Using knees was a better option because the deck beam was only supported by the width of the clamp beam, instead of the 2–3ft of a knee. There were stress concentrations over the relatively short segment of deck beam held by the clamp, and rot at the end of the deck beams could cause the deck to collapse. Yet clamps were deemed to be good enough for the year or two of a war.

Completing the hulls was paramount. While building *Lawrence* and *Niagara* Noah Brown told one carpenter: "We want no extras; plain work, plain work, is all we want. They are only required for one battle; if we win, that is all that will be wanted of them. If the enemy are victorious, the work is good enough to be captured" (quoted in Dobbins & Dobbins 1905: 324). Both sides subscribed to Brown's assessment, although American shipwrights carried it beyond that of their British counterparts. The Brown brothers, Daniel Dobbins, and Henry Eckford superintended the construction of most US-built warships on Lake Erie. Eckford completed sloop-of-war USS *General Pike*'s hull in 93 days. By 1814, he built the hulls of two frigates in an average of 72 days. The Brown brothers were swifter still, taking just 11 weeks to complete the hulls of *Lawrence* and *Niagara* – from keel-laying to launching the ships. Later, on Lake Champlain, they finished the hull of USS *Saratoga* in 35 days, and USS *Eagle* in a mere 13 days.

OCEANGOING vs. LAKES SLOOPS-OF-WAR

The difference between oceangoing sloops-of-war and those designed to sail the freshwater lakes is best illustrated by comparing the midship cross-sections of each ship. The two cross-sections (the Lakes vessel is on the left; the seagoing ship is on the right) depict 20-gun sloops-of-war of a design built in 1813. Both have roughly the same displacement and the same crew size.

Differences in the shapes of the two hulls are obvious, that of the Lakes vessel being shallower and wider than that of the oceangoing vessel. The hold of the oceangoing ship is much deeper; the Lakes vessel has less freeboard. The hold of the oceangoing ship is deep enough to allow a platform for the cable tier, where the anchor cable is stowed. With the

Lakes vessel, the cable is laid directly on the bottom of the hull because no other place for it exists.

Lakes vessels were also built differently, the frames being straighter, with less use of compass timber; and the Lakes hulls were generally assembled with more emphasis on speed than construction quality. A major difference between the two ships is the lack of knees on the Lakes vessels. The knees were "L"-shaped timbers formed where a limb joined the trunk of an oak, and were used to support the deck. On the Lakes vessels a timber was run along the side of the ship under the level of the deck, with a second one above it to "clamp" the deck to the hull.

By contrast, William M. Bell, who superintended construction of *Detroit*, took nine months to build that sloop-of-war. Work started in November 1812, following reports the Americans were building a new navy on Lake Erie. Progress was slow and *Detroit* was not fully framed until April 1813, and not launched until mid-July. Bell was no more handicapped by lack of supplies than the Brown brothers, but by the time of *Detroit*'s launch command of Lake Erie had shifted to the United States, thanks to the ships the Brown brothers built.

Quality was sacrificed for speed. Ships were pieced together with whatever wood was at hand. A bewildering mix of trees was used – elm, beech, chestnut, and pine comprised the hulls of some ships – but much of the wood was green and subject to rot. In the long run, the short run mattered more. The ships *were* required for just one battle.

THE GUNS

The ships on both sides of Lakes sloop-of-war duels were armed with the same types of weapons: smoothbore, muzzle-loading cannon. The guns were interchangeable, and in some cases guns were captured from one nation and turned against their original owners – if they were not recaptured first. Two primary types of artillery were used: long guns and carronades.

Long guns were traditional naval artillery. Made of cast iron, a long gun normally had a length 17 to 20 times the bore of the gun. Thin cast-iron cannon had a tendency to burst. To compensate, foundries cast the diameter of a gun four to five times the diameter of the bore, with the result that iron guns were heavy. Another feature was that the bore was drilled 5 percent larger than the ball it was intended to fire. This difference, called windage, compensated for irregularities in both ball and bore, preventing the ball jamming in the barrel. Windage also allowed burning gas to escape between the bore and ball, which reduced muzzle velocity and allowed the shot to bounce (or ballot) between the sides of the bore as it sped down the barrel. The gun's length compensated for these issues, forcing the ball to fly true (or at least truer) and allowing greater volume for gas expansion before the shot left the muzzle.

Guns typically fired solid-iron shot and were rated by the weight of the shot they threw. Traditional shot sizes for naval cannon were 4lb, 6lb, 9lb, 12lb, 18lb, 24lb, 32lb,

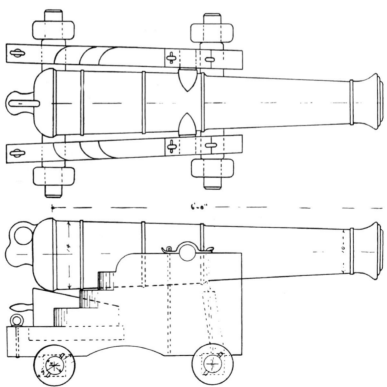

PLAN OF THE TWO LONG TWELVE-POUNDERS OF THE " NIAGARA'S " ARMAMENT

By 1813, most sloops-of-war mounted only two long guns. These were used as chase guns, when pursuing another ship. Perry's brigs mounted 12-pdr long guns such as the one shown here in overhead and side views. (AC)

THE GREAT GUNS

The three major types of guns and mountings used during the War of 1812 – carronades, long guns on pivot mounts, and long guns on naval trucked carriages – were all present on Lakes sloops-of-war and at the Battle of Lake Erie.

The carronade (**1**) was a short-barreled gun with a lug under the gun rather than the trunnions associated with standard artillery. The carronade was attached to a carriage which fitted on a slide which was fixed to the bulwark with a pivot pin. At the back of the slide, two wheels, virtually perpendicular to the slide allowed the carronade to be pivoted to a desired angle. Carronades fired heavier balls than long guns; and when the gun fired, friction absorbed recoil energy. By 1813, 32-pdr carronades were standard.

Long guns were installed on two different types of mountings. The pivot (**2**) placed the gun on a carriage fitted to a slide which rested on a large ring set on the ship's deck, pivoting on a wooden pin through the deck. Sometimes wheels were added to the slide, but frequently it sat directly on the ring, which was greased with "slush" (beef and pork fat skimmed off during cooking). When the gun fired, it recoiled back along the slide. Pivot mounts allowed one gun to fire on both sides of the ship.

The traditional trucked carriage (**3**) was also used. With this, the long gun carriage had four wooden wheels. When the gun was fired, the breeching rope absorbed much of the recoil.

and 42lb. A 12-pdr long gun fired a 12lb shot, but weighed almost 3,200lb. Sloops-of-war of the early 18th century carried main batteries of 4-pdr or 6-pdr long guns, but by the late 18th century some sloops-of-war were designed for 9-pdr main batteries. As the 19th century dawned, 12-pdr long guns began to be mounted.

The long gun's design was developed in the 1600s, and remained virtually unchanged for two centuries. In the 1770s things changed with the introduction of the carronade. Developed by the Carron Company in 1774, this completely new design was the result of improved metallurgy. It used a bore built to tighter tolerances than contemporary cannon, resulting in a tighter fit when the ball was placed. Reducing windage reduced escaping gas when the gun was fired, which meant less gunpowder was required to fire the ball. The charge was placed in a smaller chamber at the breech end of the bore. Reducing windage also reduced balloting, which meant the barrel could be shortened without sacrificing accuracy. Carron made the barrel thinner at the muzzle, further reducing the weight, thus yielding a lighter barrel. Carron cast a gun capable of firing a 24-pdr shot which weighed no more than that of a 4-pdr long gun. A 24-pdr carronade could fire that ball two-thirds the distance of the 4-pdr long gun. Mounted on a slide system to absorb part of the shock of firing, the carronade also had less recoil than conventional long guns.

Both the US Navy and the Royal Navy loved the carronade, and the 4-pdr and 6-pdr long guns on sloops-of-war were duly replaced with 24-pdr and 32-pdr carronades. They seemed unable to hit anything beyond 50yd, but naval doctrine called for fighting at close range, and sloops-of-war were fast ships capable of choosing their range. The carronade started a new round of innovation in ordnance as gun founders realized the principles applied to carronade design could be applied to other artillery. Long guns began to be cast with tighter tolerances, and new generations of medium-length guns – Blomfields, Columbaids, and other designs – began to appear by 1800.

Another innovation was the pivot mount, in which a long gun was set on a slide mount placed on a turntable. Typically located on the centerline of the ship, it could

A bow-mounted pivot on a model of a Lakes sloop-of-war from the War of 1812. Pivot guns were typically heavier than broadside guns on carriages or slides. Several ships at the Battle of Lake Erie had pivots. Some schooners were armed exclusively with them. (GG)

be turned to enable the long gun to fire off both sides. The pivot mount also enabled heavier guns to be mounted. Pivots were positioned in the center of the ship and replaced two broadside guns with one pivot gun. Thus a 20-gun sloop-of-war which might have mounted 9-pdrs for a 90lb broadside could instead mount ten 24-pdr pivots for a 240lb broadside.

THE RIGGING

All sloops-of-war were primarily sailing vessels. While many were equipped with sweeps, these were an auxiliary form of propulsion, used only when no other option was available. Darwinian selection made sloops-of-war fast sailers, especially under light winds. A sluggish sloop-of-war was quickly captured by larger warships.

Speed was achieved by multiple sails on a single mast. Masts on sloops-of-war, except the smallest, had three segments. The lower mast was anchored in the ship's hull. Attached to that was a top mast. At the top of the top mast, a third, topgallant mast was fixed. Where the top mast met the lower mast a platform, known as a fighting top, was fixed. This provided a place for sailors working the sails, and for marine sharpshooters during a battle. At the intersection of the top mast and topgallant mast, a crisscross of timbers, the crosstrees, provided a platform for the sailors working the upper sails.

Four square sails were hung from spars connected to the mast. On the lower mast, the spar for the courses (or lower sails) was positioned. This spar was fixed, and could not be moved. The topsail hung from a spar on the top mast. This spar could move from just below the crosstrees to just above the platform. The topgallant mast held two spars which held the topgallant and royal sails. On large frigates, the royal was sometimes placed on its own royal mast, above the topgallant mast, but in 1813 this feature was rare. The royal was used only during fair weather and moderate winds, and set temporarily. Both the royals and topgallant spars could be lowered.

A three-masted ship had a fore mast, main mast, and mizzen mast. A two-masted vessel generally had a fore mast and a main mast. The main mast was placed near the

The fighting top, or platform, was located where the lower mast intersected the top mast. It provided a platform to anchor the lines supporting the top mast, a place for sailors aloft to work, and a position for marine sharpshooters. Note the fixed position of the course spar and the lowered topsail spar. (GG)

point where the ship pivoted when it turned; and there was a boom ahead of the bow called the bowsprit.

The aftermost mast had a trapezoidal sail attached to the back of the lower mizzen mast. This sail, called the spanker, spencer, or gaff, helped the ship maneuver. There were also two to four triangular sails – jibs and staysails – hung from lines running from the tops of the sections of the fore mast to the bowsprit. These lines, the fore stays, helped support the fore mast. The jibs helped maneuver the ship.

The combination of sails yielding the best speed depended upon the wind direction and speed. A square-rigged sloop-of-war could generally not sail closer than 40 degrees to the direction of the wind, and generally sailed fastest when the wind was coming from about 15–60 degrees aft of the ship's beam. Unless the wind came from dead aft, it heeled the ship in the direction the wind blew. Too much heel slowed a ship because the wind started pushing the ship sideways.

By 1812 the topsails were a ship's main driving sails. In a near-calm, all sails were set. As wind speed increased, the royals were removed once a ship reached its optimal heel, then the topgallants. As wind speed increased further, the courses were reefed, and then furled completely; the topsails were then shortened.

The right mix of sails was particularly critical for Lakes sloops-of-war, with shallower hulls than their seagoing counterparts, and a higher center of gravity. With a short distance between the ship's center of gravity and the point where the hull tipped, Lakes sloops-of-war easily capsized if the wind speed increased unexpectedly. Several Lakes merchant vessels converted to warships, most notably the schooners USS *Hamilton* and USS *Scourge* in Lake Ontario, capsized during unexpected squalls.

Even in light winds, the shallow hulls worked against Lakes sloops-of-war because the keel could not grip the water well enough to sail close to the wind. This was one of the factors which caused the Battle of Lake Erie to devolve into a set of single-ship duels, rather than being a squadron action. It took a determined and skillful captain to bring a disengaged ship close enough to join the fight.

THE COMBATANTS

Despite the Lakes' strategic importance, naval forces on their waters were an afterthought. The United States and Britain initially focused naval efforts on the ocean. Even after realizing control of the Lakes represented the key to victory, both sides were parsimonious in sending sailors to man Lakes warships. Lake Erie, at the end of a long logistic chain for both sides, suffered most from manpower shortages. Commanders at Lake Ontario commanded all Lakes naval forces, and both sides tended to husband the few reinforcements they received at Lake Ontario. As a consequence, Lake Erie flotilla commanders were forced to man their ships with the few officers and men they received and any locals who would volunteer for service.

The US Navy manned its vessels with a mix of personnel recruited for the US Navy, US Marine Corps, and US Army troops willing to serve aboard US Navy ships as marines or sailors. British naval forces on the Lakes were made up of a mix of Royal Navy personnel, men and officers of the Provincial Marine, and British Army soldiers. The Provincial Marine, a maritime enforcement service organized in 1786, followed the practices and rank structure of the Royal Navy. Much like a coast guard, it was controlled by the Governor General of Canada, and run by the British Army with officers and men borrowed from the Royal Navy or recruited locally. In 1813 the Provincial Marine was absorbed into the Royal Navy.

THE MEN

Sailing ships depended upon the skills of trained mariners for efficiency. The most valued men could handle (knew the lines controlling different sails), reef (work aloft

John Chapman was a British sailor present at the Battle of Lake Erie, seconded from the Royal Navy to the Provincial Marine in 1812, before the war started. He served aboard *Queen Charlotte* as a gunner, maintop-man, and boarder. (AC)

in the masts to change the sails), and steer (manage the helm efficiently). It took at least three years' experience to gain these skills and such men were always in short supply. In the US Navy and Royal Navy a man who could perform these tasks with little supervision was rated able seaman. In 1812 over 80 percent of the able seamen were aged 30 or younger – death, disablement, and promotion removed older men from this rank. Since a sailor normally started his career in his teens, men typically served as able seamen less than a dozen years.

Ranked below able seamen were seamen (or ordinary seamen). These men had at least one year's shipboard experience and had mastered some of the skills required to sail a ship, but were still apprentices. They needed supervision to assure their work was done properly and additional experience to gain the confidence needed to act independently.

Finally, there were landsmen. These were raw recruits, unskilled and inexperienced, who could pull a rope if it was placed in their hands. There was plenty of work for these men aboard a ship because jobs requiring only brute strength were numerous. Landsmen hauled gun tackles, and handled the lines from the deck. They could man the capstan to raise the anchor and load cargo into the hold. Landsmen did not need to be mariners, so soldiers and shore-going laborers could substitute for landsmen.

Able seaman, ordinary seamen, and landsmen each comprised approximately one-third of a sloop-of-war's complement. A ship worked best with an even distribution of all three ratings, which assured a steady progression from landsman to seaman to able seaman.

A ship also had petty officers, experienced seamen given specialized leadership positions. These included coxswains (who steered the ship's boats), quartermasters (who steered the ship), and the various mates (bosun's mate, gunner's mate, carpenter's mate) and yeomen (yeoman of the sheets, yeoman of the powder room) who assisted the various warrant officers. Also numbered among petty officers were specialists such as the captain's clerk, the stewards, and sailmaker's and carpenter's crews. A sloop-of-war required at least a dozen such petty officers.

At the very bottom of the sailors' hierarchy were servants. Typically the least experienced members of the crew, they were young boys, often aged 11 to 14. A few were captain's servants intended to become midshipmen when an opening arose. Others carried gunpowder charges during battle, or did general scutwork aboard ship which required minimal strength. A sloop-of-war carried 14–20 servants.

Sloops-of-war needed crews of 120 to 160 men, including between two- and three-dozen experienced sailors for efficient operation. A sloop-of-war rated at 20 guns required a bare minimum of 12 able seamen; it was preferable to have at least 20. A 20-gun sloop-of-war also needed at least a dozen more men capable of serving as gun captains – men who knew how to aim and fire a cannon or carronade and direct the crew manning the gun. (In a pinch, gunner's mates and quarter gunners – petty officers – could fill these roles on guns without a gun captain.)

The problem on the Lakes, especially on Lake Erie, was finding the experienced sailors to man a warship. There was a core of able seamen on the Lakes as there were several dozen small merchant vessels operating on each lake during peacetime; but this was a thin leaven, for these merchant ships typically shipped crews of 9–15 men, a fraction of a sloop-of-war's crew. Britain, which had the Provincial Marine prior to the war, could draw upon the crews of these ships; but in 1812 there were fewer than six Provincial Marine vessels on the Upper Lakes (Erie, Huron, and Michigan) and fewer than six on Lake Ontario, and more than half were laid up and unmanned. The vessels in commission were undermanned, with British soldiers serving aboard. The United States was in even worse shape. It had only one warship in commission (*Oneida* on Lake Ontario), and a second ship, the brig *Detroit*, being operated by the US Army on Lake Erie to carry supplies.

Each side could draw from a pool of skilled or semiskilled sailors. For the British, *voyageurs*, who undertook long boat expeditions on the Canadian rivers, provided a pool of men familiar with watercraft, if not sails. For the United States, black sailors – many of them freemen, but undoubtedly including some runaway slaves – journeyed to the Lakes, especially Lake Erie, to serve on US Navy warships. The Northwest Territory and Pennsylvania were free. Even in New York, where slavery was still legal, officials overlooked a runaway's status if he willingly served in the US Navy. Up to one-quarter of the crew of several Lakes ships were black.

Some landsmen and servants could be recruited from the local inhabitants, but the local population was so small even landsmen were recruited from outside the Lakes. Both navies were forced to find experienced sailors from drafts on their oceangoing forces. The US Navy did a better job at this. Most of their warships were blockaded in port, and in several instances the entire crew of a trapped ship was sent to a lake to man a ship of a similar size. The sloop-of-war *Jefferson* was one such, being manned by the crew of *Erie*, a 20-gun sloop-of-war stuck in Baltimore, Maryland. In 1812 and 1813 the Royal Navy was still fighting France, as well as battling the United States. Yet it, too, sent drafts of sailors into the Lakes to man the ships being built there. Most of those men stopped at Lake Ontario. Only a trickle reached Lake Erie. When Barclay was sent to Amherstburg to take charge of Lake Erie, he was accompanied by fewer than 20 experienced seamen. *Detroit* went into battle with only ten experienced

Getting sailors to Lake Erie involved long overland journeys for both the Royal Navy and US Navy. The United States dispatched sailors from Baltimore, New York City, and various New England ports. Britain started its sailors at Quebec. (AC)

seamen, including petty officers. Other ships in Barclay's squadron had a few more, but were largely manned with soldiers and landsmen.

Perry's plight was a little better, with *Lawrence* and *Niagara* ready for action in May 1813. However, only *Lawrence* could be manned until a draft of 130 men sent by Chauncey arrived on August 9. Only after Perry received these men could he finally man and commission *Niagara* and gain naval superiority on Lake Erie.

THE OFFICERS

During the War of 1812 warships had commissioned and warrant officers. Commissioned officers received commissions from their governments – the British Crown through the Admiralty for the Royal Navy and the President of the United States for the US Navy. Warrant officers held their office by virtue of a warrant appointing them to their position. In the Royal Navy the Board of the Admiralty issued warrants. In the US Navy, the Navy Department issued warrants. Commissioned officers ran the warship, and held ultimate responsibility for its fighting efficiency, safety, and navigation. Warrant officers were senior specialists responsible for specific aspects of the ship requiring a high level of knowledge and experience. Commissioned officers, even a lieutenant with the ink still damp on his commission, outranked a ship's most senior warrant officer.

The divide between commissioned officers and warrant officers dated back to when civilian ships were commandeered for naval service. Commissioned officers were in charge of fighting the ship (including any soldiers aboard), while warrant officers represented the men who ran the operations of the ship while a merchant vessel. Over time the commissioned officers had transformed from soldiers at sea into true naval officers, while the warrant officers became permanently appointed specialists still concerned with operating the ship.

There were three basic commissioned ranks in 1813: lieutenant, commander (or master commandant in the US Navy), and captain. Above these were flag ranks – the various admirals who commanded groups of ships. Lieutenant was the most junior commissioned rank. A lieutenant was capable of navigating a ship, running a watch (running a ship during a two- or four-hour shift), and commanding a battery of guns (generally one broadside on one deck) during combat. Lieutenants might even command small warships. In both the Royal Navy and US Navy a lieutenant was expected to have at least six years' experience at sea, either as a midshipman (an apprentice officer) or a master's mate (training to navigate a ship). They were typically promoted from the ranks of the most capable officer trainees, although influence (social or family connections) hastened promotion. Even those promoted through influence tended to be competent, however. Captains had to sleep sometimes, and they slept sounder in the knowledge that their watch officer was capable of keeping the ship off reefs and shoals.

While some lieutenants were newly made, many had years of experience. Promotion in a peacetime navy or one which was not growing (as was the case for the Royal Navy *c.*1805–15) could be slow, especially for officers lacking influence or an opportunity

OLIVER HAZARD PERRY

Oliver Hazard Perry was born August 23, 1785 in South Kingston, Rhode Island, the eldest child of Christopher Raymond Perry and Sarah Wallace Perry (née Alexander). He had four siblings, including Matthew Calbraith Perry, a future commodore in the US Navy.

Perry came from a naval family. His father served on a privateer in the American Revolutionary War, commanded merchant ships following that war, and received a captain's commission in the US Navy when it was reestablished in 1799. Perry sailed aboard his father's cargo ship at age 12, and joined the US Navy as a midshipman in April 1799 at age 13. During the Quasi-War with France in 1799–1801, Perry served aboard the frigate USS *General Greene* (commanded by his father), seeing service in the West Indies. During the First Barbary War (1801–05) Perry served aboard the frigate USS *Adams* in the Mediterranean during its 1802–03 cruise. Perry remained with the American Mediterranean squadron, receiving promotion to acting lieutenant in 1805. Given command of USS *Nautilus*, a 12-gun vessel then rigged as a schooner, he participated in the capture of Derna in 1805, supporting marines landing there under command of Lieutenant Presley O'Bannon.

Returning to the United States in 1806, Perry was placed on leave through 1807. In 1807 he received his commission as a lieutenant, and was assigned to oversee construction of the portion of President Thomas Jefferson's gunboat flotillas being built in New England. On April 12, 1809 he was given command of USS *Revenge*, another 12-gun schooner. He enforced the Embargo Act off the Carolinas. In 1810, *Revenge* was sent to New England and Perry ordered to conduct harbor surveys. *Revenge* ran aground off Rhode Island in January 1811 and was wrecked. Perry was court-martialed for the loss of the ship and acquitted. Given a leave of absence after the court martial, he married Elizabeth Champlin Mason of Newport, Rhode Island on May 5, 1811. They would have five children, one of whom died in infancy.

Perry was not actively employed by the US Navy until after the War of 1812 started. In August 1812 he was promoted to master commandant; but despite numerous requests for active service, he remained unemployed. Isaac Chauncey, a friend with whom Perry served in the Mediterranean, was appointed to command naval forces in the Great Lakes. Perry wrote him, requesting employment. Chauncey had Perry sent to Lake Ontario in February 1813 to superintend the construction of two 20-gun brigs and to command the US Navy's squadron on Lake Erie. Perry's efforts led to the construction of a squadron superior to that of the Royal Navy, and eventually to a decisive American victory at the Battle of Lake Erie. As a result, Perry was promoted to captain in November 1813, backdated to September 10, 1813, the date of the battle.

In July 1814 Captain Perry was appointed to command the 44-gun frigate USS *Java*, then under construction in Baltimore, Maryland. While superintending the completion of *Java*, Perry participated in the defense of Baltimore and Washington, DC during the summer British invasion of Chesapeake Bay in September 1814. *Java*, completed in 1815, was sent to the Mediterranean under Perry's command with one of two US Navy squadrons sent to settle affairs with the Barbary States. In April 1815 he landed at Algiers and concluded a peace treaty. Perry returned to the United States in 1817 and in October that year fought a duel with the officer who had been Marine Lieutenant aboard *Java*, and was challenged to a duel by Jesse Elliott, his second-in-command at Lake Erie.

In 1819 Perry was placed in command of anti-piracy efforts in the West Indies. After visiting Venezuela, Perry contracted yellow fever. He died from the disease August 23, 1819.

A romanticized painting of Oliver Hazard Perry at the Battle of Lake Erie. (LOC)

ROBERT HERIOT BARCLAY

Born September 18, 1786, in Kettle, Scotland, Robert Heriot Barclay was the second son of a Scots minister. He entered the Royal Navy in May 1798 at age 11 and served as a midshipman aboard HMS *Anson*, one of three 44-gun frigates cut down from 64-gun ships-of-the-line. In February 1805 he was transferred to Lord Nelson's flagship, HMS *Victory*.

One month later he was promoted to acting lieutenant, and posted aboard the 74-gun ship-of-the-line HMS *Swiftsure*. His promotion was confirmed on October 11, 1805, ten days before the Battle of Trafalgar where he fought as a lieutenant aboard *Swiftsure*. Following the battle he was instrumental in rescuing 170 sailors from the captured French ship-of-the-line *Redoutable*, which had been captured as a prize and was under tow by *Swiftsure*. *Redoutable* sank in the storm following the battle.

In 1808 Barclay was appointed second lieutenant in the 38-gun frigate HMS *Diana*, during its fourth commission under Captain Charles Grant. In November 1809, while leading a cutting-out party against a French convoy, he was injured and lost his left arm. In 1810 he was sent to the North American station, where he expected promotion to commander. Instead, between July 1810 and October 1812 Barclay briefly commanded the schooner HMS *Bream* as a lieutenant, and served as a lieutenant aboard the 32-gun frigate HMS *Aeolus*, the 16-gun ship-sloop HMS *Tartarus*, and HMS *Iphigenia*, a 38-gun frigate in European waters.

In February 1813, Barclay was sent to Halifax, the senior lieutenant of a small group of naval officers sent to the Lakes. On May 5, he arrived in Kingston, the British naval station on Lake Ontario. He briefly served as acting commander of all British naval forces on the Lakes, before being superseded by the arrival of Captain Sir James Lucas Yeo, who ordered Barclay to take command of British naval forces on Lake Erie. Barclay was not Yeo's first choice, this command having first been offered to Captain William Howe Mulcaster, the next in command to Yeo, who declined. Barclay arrived at Amherstburg, on the western end of Lake Erie on June 5, and took command of the small squadron there. For the next four months he attempted to maintain British control of Lake Erie, a task made more difficult after the commissioning of *Niagara* and *Lawrence* in July and August.

On September 9, Barclay took his squadron against the US Navy squadron led by Oliver Hazard Perry. The next day, September 10, the two squadrons fought off the Bass

Robert Heriot Barclay. This painting shows him as a captain, years after the Battle of Lake Erie. (AC)

Islands in western Lake Erie, where Barclay's entire squadron was captured. Barclay was badly wounded during the battle, losing part of his remaining arm and a leg. Despite the loss, he was promoted to commander on November 19, 1813. In August 1814, he married his first cousin, Agnes Cosser. The marriage produced several children.

Court-martialed for the loss of his ship at the Battle of Lake Erie in September 1814, Barclay was honorably acquitted. The court decided the loss was due to "the very defective means" Barclay had available to outfit and man his squadron. Canadians remembered his efforts with a gift of plate, and on November 7, 1815, the Admiralty granted Barclay an annual pension of £200 in addition to the five pence per day he was allowed for his wounds. Despite his injuries Barclay began petitioning the Admiralty for employment in 1822. He was given command of the bomb-vessel HMS *Infernal* in April 1824, remaining in command until October 1824, when he was promoted to captain. He received no active employment in the Royal Navy after that date, remaining on half-pay until his death on May 8, 1837.

to distinguish themselves. When multiple lieutenants were present (a ship-of-the-line might have seven) they sorted themselves out by seniority, with the officer holding a commission longest first among equals.

The next step up was commander (or master commandant in the US Navy). This rank emerged in the mid-18th century as an intermediate step between lieutenant and captain, with promotion usually based on meritorious service or influence. The rank permitted younger but (theoretically) more capable officers the opportunity to command a ship too small for a captain, but large enough to require more than one commissioned officer. A commander typically had charge of a 16- to 22-gun sloop-of-war.

Above commander/master commandant was captain. A captain commanded a ship of 24 or more guns. Sloops-of-war were small ships generally with three or fewer commissioned officers, belonging to the two lowest ranks of commissioned officer – lieutenant and commander/master commandant. At Lake Erie, all officers commanding sloops-of-war were lieutenants, with the exception of Perry and Elliott who were master commandants. *Detroit* and *Queen Charlotte* were ships which should have been captained by commanders, but the 1812 Royal Navy awarded rank parsimoniously.

The warrant officers were in charge of different aspects of running the ship. Ships had at least five warrant officers: the master was responsible for navigation; the boatswain (or bosun) held responsibility for a ship's masts, rigging, sails, anchors, and cables, and maintaining discipline among the crew; the carpenter was in charge of hull maintenance and repair; the gunner tended the ship's armament; and the purser took charge of supplies – food, clothing, and stores. In addition a ship's surgeon, chaplain, schoolmaster, and cook were accorded the status of warrant officers, although sloops-of-war rarely carried chaplains or schoolmasters. Masters were accorded the status of lieutenants, often messed with the lieutenants, and commanded warships too small for lieutenants.

Between the commissioned and warrant officers were the midshipmen, apprentice officers. Considered gentlemen, they were expected to work in the rigging with the common sailors. It was an anomalous position. In theory a midshipman ranked a warrant officer, but it took a very brash or very experienced midshipman to attempt this. In battle a midshipman would take charge of a section of guns (often four) under the supervision of a lieutenant, or perhaps run the men in a fighting top.

Both nations drew their commissioned officers, warrant officers, and midshipmen from the same classes of people. Officers came from the gentry or the professional classes. They were literate, could handle upper mathematics required for navigation, and were generally propertied. Warrant officers were drawn from seafaring families, often from the merchant service but equally from the more capable forecastle hands. Midshipmen generally came from the same class as the officers, but a large minority – as much as one-third – came from seafaring backgrounds. Both navies were meritocracies in 1812; capable people were too rare to waste. This would change during the long peace following 1815, but in 1813 intelligent and able seamen still had the chance to end a career as a captain.

THE MARINES

Naval warships of the age of fighting sail generally carried a contingent of marines. The marines were sea soldiers, trained and drilled as soldiers, but capable of fighting from ships. They served three major functions. In naval combat they served as snipers and sharpshooters. Marines were stationed in the ship's fighting tops, and along the forecastle and quarterdeck bulwarks to pick off enemy officers and gunners. They were also used for boarding battles as seagoing infantry.

Marines also were used for any combat activities ashore. When raiding a port, attacking a shore battery or signal station, or if the need temporarily arose to occupy fortifications ashore, the marine contingent of a ship was landed. They would serve as infantry where infantry was needed.

Finally, the marines provided seagoing discipline. The marines were berthed between the crew and the officers, providing separation. They provided the sentries at

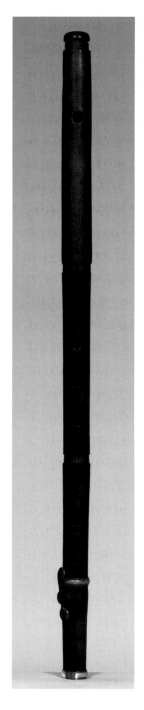

Warships were homes as well as fighting platforms. This one-key flute was carried during the campaign by Jeff Selden, a Battle of Lake Erie veteran, who entertained himself and his comrades with it in their off-hours. (LOC)

Reenactors dressed in the uniform of the Royal Newfoundland Regiment marching during a War of 1812 bicentennial event. During the Battle of Lake Erie, 40 members of the regiment were killed or taken prisoner. (Courtesy Royal Newfoundland Regiment Museum)

hatches and doorways to ensure only those authorized to enter passed. In the event of mutinous behavior by the sailors the marines could be armed and turned out to restore order.

Sloops-of-war were intended to carry a marine contingent of 30–45 men, but the number of marines allocated depended upon the size of the ship. Typically, the contingent consisted of a marine lieutenant, a sergeant, and a corporal with 25 to 40 privates. Both the US Navy and the Royal Navy had dedicated marine forces: the United States Marine Corps and the Royal Marines, respectively. As with everything else on the Lakes – especially Lake Erie – both sides experienced difficulties filling their marine contingents with men from the US Marine Corps or the Royal Marines. The Royal Marines contingent on Lake Erie was non-existent. Things were a little better for the United States, but only barely. A marine lieutenant, John Brooks, Jr., was sent from Washington, DC to Erie with a recruiting party of seven enlisted marines. By the time he arrived at Erie he had added seven privates. He recruited an additional 20 men at Erie, yielding a total of 35 marines to spread among Perry's ships.

Both sides made up their marine shortfalls with soldiers. Major General William Henry Harrison, commanding US Army forces in the Northwestern United States, provided Perry with nearly 100 volunteers from Ohio and Kentucky militia units. Barclay manned his ships with 160 soldiers: 54 from the Royal Newfoundland Fencibles and 106 from the British Army's 41st Regiment of Foot. The soldiers substituted for sailors in addition to serving as marines, and many filled positions which should have been taken by landsmen.

Ohio militiamen, many of whom had worked on boats on Ohio rivers during peacetime, were used as sailors. The buckskin-clad Kentucky militia soldiers, completely unfamiliar with watercraft, were used to fill out the ranks of marines. *Lawrence* used the United States Marine Corps contingent recruited by Brooks, Jr., who served as the marine lieutenant. Kentucky militia provided the marine contingents for Perry's other ships.

Barclay filled the marine detachments of his ships with the Royal Newfoundland Regiment. Five companies of the Royal Newfoundland Regiment, many of whom were expert boatmen, had been sent to the Lakes to serve as marines on Barclay's warships. Troops of the 41st Foot, some without their red coats, served as landsmen aboard Barclay's ships, hauling the gun tackles.

Although the quota of actual marines on the Lakes was small, and virtually negligible at the Battle of Lake Erie, soldiers did fight aboard Lakes warships. Simply because of their presence, and the manpower they provided working the ships' great guns, they played an important role at the Battle of Lake Erie.

COMBAT

Over three years of warfare on the Great Lakes and Lake Champlain, numerous battles were fought, but few were decisive. Of the minor battles fought on the Lakes, the only decisive actions in which ships were captured were due to cutting-out operations, vessels running aground within range of shore batteries, or raids on naval bases. Most common were cutting-out operations, where parties of armed sailors and marines took small boats to capture vessels anchored offshore. The United States captured *Detroit* and *Caledonia* that way in 1812, and in 1814, lost USS *Scorpion* and USS *Tigress* in Georgian Bay, and USS *Ohio* and USS *Somers* off Fort Erie in two separate cutting-out actions on Lake Huron and Lake Erie, respectively. None of the ships cut out were major warships, mounting 12 or more guns. Most were schooners converted from civilian use and armed with one to three guns. *Detroit* and *Caledonia* were small brigs. None displaced more than 125 tons, most weighing in at 60 tons.

Of battles involving squadrons of ships – six or more per side – only the Battle of Lake Erie and Battle of Lake Champlain were decisive. The half-dozen major actions on Lake Ontario were skirmishes where neither side proved willing to risk all for a major victory. There were a few single-ship actions fought as part of these battles, the most notable being a battle between the 22-gun HMS *Wolfe* and the 26-gun *General Pike*. Yet generally, as soon as one ship began to be bettered by the other, it retreated to the safety of its fleet or shore batteries. Unless an urgent reason existed to push for victory, both British and American commanders were willing to wait for a better opportunity.

The necessity to fight existed at both the Battle of Lake Erie and the Battle of Lake Champlain. Although weaker than Perry, Barclay was running out of food and needed a victory to regain control of Lake Erie. Waiting for a better opportunity meant he might be starved out before it came. At Lake Champlain, Royal Navy

control of the lake was essential to support a British invasion of New York. The US Navy equally needed control of Lake Champlain to stop a British army from moving into New York.

At the Battle of Lake Champlain both sides fought coordinated battles, with a line of battle. Moreover, the action was fought from anchor. The Battle of Lake Erie was a sailing action, with both flotillas moving under sail. Although both commanders intended to fight a coordinated action, the battle did not work out that way. Due to light winds, ill-trained crews, and sluggish captains, the battle devolved into a series of single-ship actions. Although other ships were present and contributed to the outcome, the battle was decided by a fight between *Lawrence* and *Detroit* followed by a duel between *Niagara* and *Detroit*. All three were sloops-of-war, as were other participants, namely the ship-sloop HMS *Queen Charlotte*, the brigs USS *Caledonia* and HMS *General Hunter*, and the 12-gun schooner HMS *Lady Prevost*. These two actions between sloops-of-war in the waters north of Put-in-Bay on Lake Erie highlighted both the strengths and weaknesses of this class of warship, particularly Lakes sloops-of-war.

THE PATH TO BATTLE

The Battle of Lake Erie really started in September 1812. The United States' presence on Lake Erie or the other Upper Lakes was then non-existent. The British had one 20-gun ship-sloop, *Queen Charlotte*, a ten-gun brig-sloop, *General Hunter*, and a newly finished schooner, *Lady Prevost*, carrying 13 guns: three long guns and ten 12-pdr carronades. These three ships were built for and manned by the Provincial Marine.

In addition, the brig *Caledonia* had been commandeered from the Canadian North West Company, the brig *Adams* captured from the US Army, and three schooners captured from American companies. These ships were hastily armed. *Adams*, renamed *Detroit*, carried six 6-pdr long guns. The rest – *Caledonia*, *Erie*, *Little Belt*, and *Chippawa* – were each armed with one to three guns. All were lightly manned. Since the United States had no warships, deficiency in manpower mattered little.

In September 1812 Captain Isaac Chauncey, commanding United States naval forces on the Lakes, sent Lieutenant Jesse Elliott to Black Rock, New York with instructions to open a naval base and build a flotilla to challenge the British. Black Rock, a village on the Niagara River with access to Lake Erie, had little but the virtue of being close to Lake Ontario to recommend it. It was small, on the border, and ill-suited as a shipyard. Upon arrival Elliott discovered two British warships, *Caledonia* and *Detroit*, anchored off Fort Erie, on the Canadian side of the Niagara. On October 8, 1812 Elliott took the men he had, put them in boats, and captured the two ships. During the attempt to take them to Black Rock, however, *Detroit* ran aground and was burned to prevent recapture. *Caledonia* arrived safely, becoming the first American warship on Lake Erie. Winter ended further campaigning, but between November 1812 and March 1813 Elliott purchased four civilian schooners laid up at Black Rock.

Over the same period Daniel Dobbins convinced the Navy Department that Presque Isle was a better place for a naval shipyard on Lake Erie. By December Dobbins had two schooners framed, but after a visit by Chauncey in January 1813, he lengthened two other schooners then being built and began preliminary work to

A model of the brig USS *Adams*, used by the US Army prior to the War of 1812. Taken by the British when Detroit was captured, it was put into British service as HMS *Detroit*. Later, as *Detroit*, it was captured on the Niagara River by Lieutenant Jesse Elliott and his men. *Detroit* subsequently ran aground and was burned to prevent British recapture. (USNHHC)

"LAKE FEVER"

When the Battle of Lake Erie was fought, 116 of Perry's 532 men were ill with "lake fever." Some claim lake fever was malaria or yellow fever. Both are transmitted by mosquitoes, which plague the Great Lakes. Another cause of lake fever lay in the various diseases transmitted through drinking water contaminated with protozoa, amoeba, and bacteria.

The freshwater Great Lakes simplify the task of obtaining drinking water. In the early 19th century the lakes themselves were largely unpolluted and offered safe drinking water. Indeed, Lake freighters drew drinking water, unfiltered, from Lake Superior into the 1970s. Crews filling water kegs straight from Lake Erie a few miles upstream of their anchorage would have been safe. However, many ships drew water directly from the harbor where they anchored – water into which raw sewage had been dumped. The germ theory of disease still lay in the future. The water appeared good. It was clearer than water long stored in the barrel on oceangoing voyages, and it tasted untainted. Yet it was deadly.

Since lake water was fresh, Perry's ships drew drinking water directly from their anchorages, such as this one. While the water tasted clean, it was contaminated. (LOC)

build two 300-ton brigs. By mid-February 1813 Dobbins was joined by two other shipbuilders, Noah and Adam Brown, accompanied by a core of 15 carpenters and blacksmiths to build the new brigs. In late March, Master Commandant Oliver Hazard Perry arrived at Erie to command the squadron building there. He brought 150 sailors with him to man the ships.

Alarmed at reports of American naval activity, Provincial Marine officials at Amherstburg began work on a new ship-sloop. Authorized in November 1812, work did not start until the following January. The ship, christened *Detroit*, was a copy of *Queen Charlotte*. It was finally launched in August 1813.

This escalating battle continued through the spring of 1813, and the US led the race. The Brown brothers achieved prodigies, with both of their brigs in the water by May. Chauncey sent Henry Eckford to Black Rock to outfit the five ships Elliott had gathered there. Eckford armed each of them with one or two pivot-mounted guns in record time. Perry, an energetic commander, brought scarce items such as iron fittings and cannon to remote Erie in time to finish the building of the warships there.

The British response was more muted. No resources were sent to Lake Erie until May 1813. Until then, the Provincial Marine made do with what they had. Their officers and men were capable enough, but the Provincial Marine had doubled the number of ships in commission when the war started. Not until May did Captain Sir James Lucas Yeo send reinforcements – Barclay, a few Royal Navy lieutenants, and a handful of sailors. Barclay finally arrived at Amherstburg on June 5 in the knowledge that the two big US brigs would outclass his entire squadron. Either one could beat *Queen Charlotte*, *General Hunter*, and *Lady Prevost* unaided; together they would

OPPOSITE Significant events on Lake Erie during 1812 and 1813. The Battle of Lake Erie was the culmination of actions taken over the first two years of the conflict.

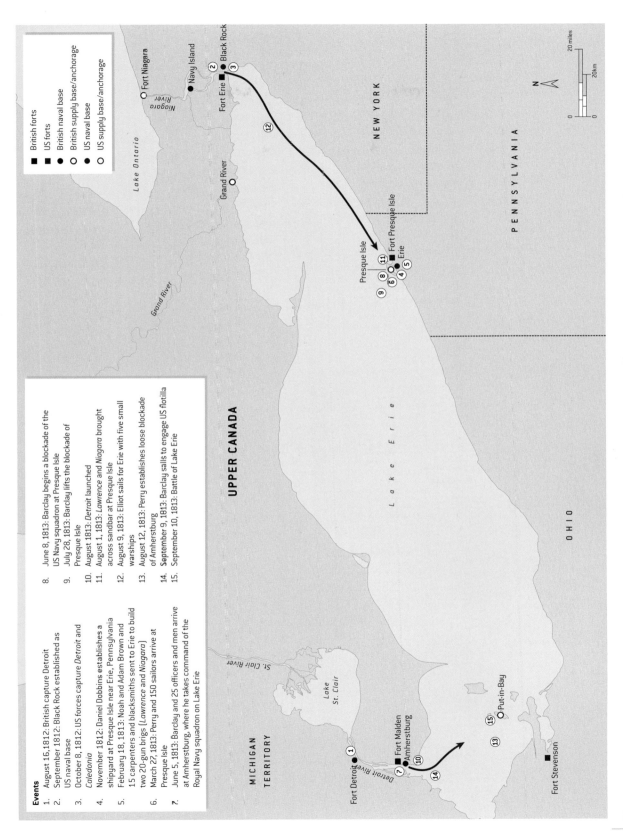

Events

1. August 16,1812: British capture Detroit
2. September 1812: Black Rock established as US naval base
3. October 8, 1812: US forces capture *Detroit* and *Caledonia*
4. November 1812: Daniel Dobbins establishes a shipyard at Presque Isle near Erie, Pennsylvania
5. February 18, 1813: Noah and Adam Brown and 15 carpenters and blacksmiths sent to Erie to build two 20-gun brigs (*Lawrence* and *Niagara*)
6. March 27, 1813: Perry and 150 sailors arrive at Presque Isle
7. June 5, 1813: Barclay and 25 officers and men arrive at Amherstburg, where he takes command of the Royal Navy squadron on Lake Erie
8. June 8, 1813: Barclay begins a blockade of the US Navy squadron at Presque Isle
9. July 28, 1813: Barclay lifts the blockade of Presque Isle
10. August 1813: *Detroit* launched
11. August 1, 1813: *Lawrence* and *Niagara* brought across sandbar at Presque Isle
12. August 9, 1813: Elliot sails for Erie with five small warships
13. August 12, 1813: Perry establishes loose blockade of Amherstburg
14. **September** 9, 1813: Barclay sails to engage US flotilla
15. September 10, 1813: Battle of Lake Erie

Legend:
- British forts
- US forts
- British naval base
- British supply base/anchorage
- US naval base
- US supply base/anchorage

53

Lieutenant Jesse Elliott was originally in charge of US naval forces on Lake Erie until superseded by the more senior Oliver Hazard Perry. Elliott was promoted to master commandant in July 1813, and given command of *Niagara* after joining Perry at Erie. (AC)

doom the British. Both brigs had been launched, but were in Presque Isle Bay, trapped there by a sandbar. To cross the sandbar they would first have to be disarmed and emptied of all ballast and stores.

Barclay's best plan would have been to invade the Presque Isle shipyard and burn it. It was vulnerable to attack, the US Army garrison being too weak and misplaced. Unfortunately, Barclay's British Army counterpart refused to supply troops for the attempt, so Barclay decided to keep the brigs bottled up in the bay by blockading Erie. If the two brigs crossed the sandbar with Barclay waiting outside, he could pounce and destroy them. Three days after he arrived at Amherstburg Barclay had his ships at sea, blockading Presque Isle. They waited seven weeks. Perry was unwilling to risk his ships while Barclay lay offshore. He waited, too. Finally, low on supplies, Barclay lifted the blockade on July 30, returning to Amherstburg for replenishment. He was back by August 4, but it appeared to be too late: both *Lawrence* and *Niagara* were outside the sandbar, in Lake Erie, apparently armed.

In reality, the ships had just crossed the sandbar and were in fact unready to fight. Nevertheless, Perry carefully created the impression he was ready to attack Barclay's force. Barclay folded his hand, retreating to Amherstburg to await the completion of *Detroit*. Perry followed two days later, but failed to find Barclay. Perry then returned to Erie to load provisions for the American army at Sandusky, Ohio. There he discovered reinforcements: Jesse Elliott (promoted to master commandant in July), Elliott's five warships from Black Rock, and 120 sailors.

Perry spent the next few days reorganizing his flotilla. Elliott was given *Niagara*. One of the Black Rock schooners was left at Erie, too decayed for service. The other ten ships – *Lawrence* and *Niagara*, the brig *Caledonia*, and schooners *Ariel*, *Scorpion*, *Somers*, *Ohio*, *Porcupine*, *Tigress*, and *Trippe* – sailed for Sandusky on August 12. The United States now controlled Lake Erie. Perry stationed his force at Put-in-Bay, in the Bass Islands in western Lake Erie; the anchorage offered excellent access to Amherstburg, which was blockaded. The key loss due to the blockade for the British was provisions. The British had been moving food from Lower Canada by lake and buying food from Ohio farmers. In addition to feeding British Army and naval forces, the British were also expected to provide food for several thousand indigenous allies who would leave if unfed. By early September Amherstburg was almost out of food. On September 9, with *Detroit* added to his force, Barclay sailed from Amherstburg, to meet and defeat the American squadron.

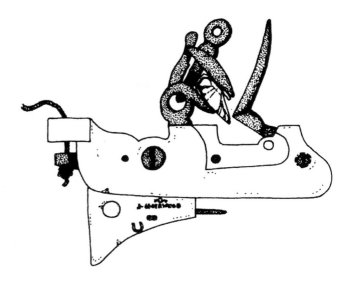

A drawing of a British cannon lock from the War of 1812. Sparks created by striking flint to steel touched off the priming gunpowder in the cannon's vent. Barclay lacked the number of cannon locks needed to equip *Detroit*'s guns. (KC)

OPENING MOVES

The fleet Barclay took out of Amherstburg was ill-assorted. Leading was *Chippawa*, a small 70-ton schooner armed with a single pivot-mounted 9-pdr long gun. It had been captured at Michilimackinac in 1812, and had a crew of 16 aboard.

The flagship *Detroit* was next, so new its paint had barely dried. *Detroit* was manned by a crew of 150, which had been pulled together only a few days earlier. While Barclay had first call on a draft of 36 sailors which arrived September 5, the majority of the crew comprised landsmen, and they had worked together only a few days. Naval stores and artillery needed to complete *Detroit* never arrived (guns intended for *Detroit* were captured at York when Chauncey took the British base in May), so it had to be equipped with a suite of spare sails from *Queen Charlotte* and guns taken from Fort Malden. As a result its guns were a mishmash of sizes and types. Many lacked flintlocks. A few had to be fired using linstocks – a slow match on a long stick, long since eclipsed on naval guns by flintlocks. Others had to be fired by flashing pistols over the cannon's touchhole. Flashing involved holding the pistol over the cannon's vent with the pistol's lock over the touchhole. When the pistol's trigger was pulled, the spark from the pistol's lock hopefully ignited the cannon's priming gunpowder. Firing through flashing involved standing beside the cannon. If you were successful and the cannon fired, it then recoiled, crushing your feet if they were in the path of recoil.

Perry made Put-in-Bay on South Bass Island his fleet anchorage while blockading Amherstburg. Lookouts spotted Barclay's flotilla from US ships anchored there. (AC)

The brig *General Hunter* was next in line. Displacing 180 tons, with a crew of 45, it was indifferently armed. It carried two 6-pdr long guns, four 4-pdr long guns, two 12-pdr carronades, and a pair of 2-pdr popguns. Its broadside was only 28lb. *Queen Charlotte*, a near-sister to *Detroit*, followed. Displacing 400 tons, the previous year it carried 20 guns: four 12-pdr long guns and 16 24-pdr carronades. Its battery had since been lightened, however, perhaps to arm other ships. At Lake Erie, *Queen Charlotte* carried three 12-pdr long guns (one on a pivot) and 14 24-pdr carronades. It had 130 men aboard, but fewer than 15 were seamen.

Bringing up the rear were the schooner *Lady Prevost* and the sloop *Little Belt*. *Lady Prevost* had been built as a warship. It displaced 230 tons, carried 86 men, and was armed with three 9-pdr long guns (one pivot-mounted) and ten 12-pdr carronades. Tiny *Little Belt* had been captured at Michilimackinac, displaced 90 tons, had a crew of 18, and was armed with one 9-pdr and two 6-pdr long guns.

Perry's fleet was anchored in Put-in-Bay on the day Barclay's fleet sailed from Amherstburg. Barclay was sailing in line ahead to the southwest, when at 7:00am on September 10, lookouts aboard *Lawrence* spotted the line of British ships 10 miles to the west. The wind was light, blowing from the southeast to the northwest. Perry was missing one ship: the schooner *Ohio* was absent. Only 416 of the 532 men mustered on his ships were available for duty. The rest, over 20 percent, were on the sick list. Yet Perry's fleet was still significantly stronger than Barclay's. Perry ordered the anchors weighed, and sailed to meet the foe. One additional factor favored Perry – the wind shifted from southeast to southwest as his ships stood out of harbor. This placed him upwind of Barclay, allowing Perry to choose his distance.

The winds were light and fluky, and it was not until 10:00am that Perry's fleet cleared Rattlesnake Island, 2 miles northwest of Put-in-Bay. Once in open water, Perry's ships cleared for action, striking unnecessary material below and preparing for battle, forming a line of battle.

"CAPTAIN" PERRY AND "CAPTAIN" BARCLAY

A sloop-of-war is a command for a lieutenant or a commander. At Lake Erie, Barclay was a lieutenant, while Perry was a master commandant. Both were the senior officer for their stations. Perry became a captain in November 1813 (backdated to September 10, 1813), while Barclay achieved that rank in 1824. Many accounts of the Battle of Lake Erie refer to Perry and Barclay as captains or commodores. Several period paintings of the battle depict them in captain's uniforms, including the famous painting of Perry rowed to *Niagara*, which has him in a full-dress captain's uniform.

The reason lies in naval custom. The officer commanding a warship is accorded the title "captain," regardless of his actual rank or the ship's size. Similarly, the senior officer commanding a squadron was often accorded the title "commodore" to distinguish him from fellow officers of similar ranks. These courtesy titles did not change the individual's actual rank, pay, or uniform, but those outside the Navy often did not realize this.

Perry was not wearing a full-dress uniform during the Battle of Lake Erie. Rather, this plain jacket was what he had on. [AC]

In the lead were two of the schooners Dobbins built at Erie: *Ariel* followed by *Scorpion*. *Ariel* was Perry's biggest schooner, at 112 tons. It carried four 12-pdr long guns, all on pivots, and 36 men. *Scorpion*, smaller at 86 tons, carried one 24-pdr long gun, one 32-pdr carronade, and a crew of 35. Behind these was the flagship *Lawrence*, Perry in command. At nearly 500 tons it was bigger than the ship-rigged *Detroit* and *Queen Charlotte*. It mounted 18 32-pdr carronades and two 12-pdr long guns. It needed 160 men to be fully manned, but only had 136 signed on – and over 30 of those absent due to illness.

USS *Caledonia*, 86 tons with 53 men aboard, followed. It carried two 12-pdr long guns and one 32-pdr carronade, all mounted on pivots. It had a broadside of 56lb, but the brig was a ponderous sailer. *Caledonia* was followed by *Niagara*, a twin to *Lawrence*. *Niagara* was commanded by Jesse Elliott and had a crew of 125 effectives and 28 men on the sick list, not aboard. The positioning of the weak, sluggish *Caledonia* was curious. Possibly Perry placed it there so it would be opposite the equally weak *General Hunter*, placing *Lawrence* across from *Detroit* and *Niagara* opposing *Queen Charlotte*. As long as the captain of each United States ship focused on the ship his vessel was supposed to be fighting, the arrangement made sense.

In line ahead behind *Niagara* were four more schooners: *Tigress, Trippe, Somers*, and *Porcupine*. *Tigress* and *Porcupine* were sister ships built by Dobbins. Each displaced 52 tons, and carried a single 32-pdr pivot-mounted long gun. *Tigress* had 27 men aboard; *Porcupine* 25. *Somers* and *Trippe* were purchased at Black Rock. *Somers* was 65 tons, had a crew of 30, and mounted two pivot-mounted guns: a 24-pdr long gun

It took 30 minutes from the time *Detroit* opened fire until *Lawrence* was close enough to use its carronades effectively. Once within range, *Detroit* and *Lawrence* traded broadsides until both had been reduced to wrecks. (USNHHC)

and a 32-pdr carronade. *Trippe* was 60 tons, had a single pivot-mounted 24-pdr long gun, and 35 men. These four ships were capable of overwhelming the trailing pair of British ships.

The wind continued light, providing a challenge to the raw crews on both sides. The wind favored Perry as he closed. Barclay's line was sailing close-hauled. Perry's closing angle put the wind on his beam. Finally, at 11:45am, *Detroit* opened the action, firing a single shot from its 24-pdr long gun.

BATTLE PHASE I: *LAWRENCE* vs. *DETROIT*

Detroit's first shot fell short, after which the two lines of ships slowly drifted together. The two flotillas were on near-parallel courses, with a closing angle of 15 degrees. In the light winds the ships moved at the speed of a walking man, and every minute brought the two lines 20–25yd closer. Five minutes later, *Detroit* fired its port-side 24-pdr long gun once again. This time the ball reached *Lawrence*. *Scorpion*, ahead of *Lawrence*, responded with its lone 32-pdr pivot carronade. During this interval Perry had *Lawrence*'s port bow-chaser, a 12-pdr long gun, shifted to the starboard side. This gave him two 12-pdrs with range enough to reach *Detroit*. At 11:55am, the 12-pdrs opened fire. At noon *Lawrence*'s starboard carronades joined the 12-pdrs, but the first broadside proved ineffectual.

Meanwhile the action became general. *Caledonia* marked *General Hunter* as its target. *Caledonia*'s long guns allowed it to hammer the lightly armed *General Hunter*, whose return fire with light guns was ineffectual. *Niagara* and *Queen Charlotte* squared off against each other, but at a range where neither ship's carronades were effectual. *Niagara* was only reaching *Queen Charlotte* with a single 12-pdr long gun while *Queen Charlotte* replied with two. Meanwhile *Tigress*, *Trippe*, *Porcupine*, and *Somers* concentrated fire on *Lady Prevost* and *Little Belt*.

OPPOSITE Ship movements during the Battle of Lake Erie. What appears at first glance to be a coordinated squadron action can be better understood as a set of closely spaced single-ship actions.

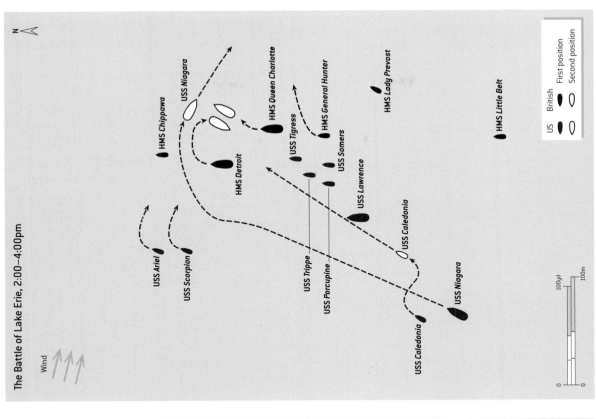

The Battle of Lake Erie, 2:00–4:00pm

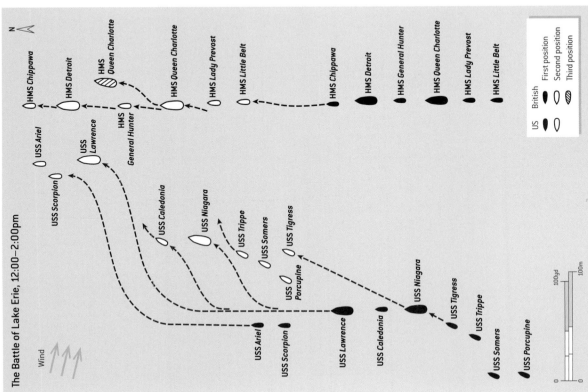

The Battle of Lake Erie, 12:00–2:00pm

QUARTERDECK VIEW: USS *LAWRENCE*

When *Lawrence* opened fire at 11:55am it could only hit *Detroit* with its two 12-pdr bow-chasers, which were long guns. Because of the shallow angle at which the two ships closed, it took nearly 40 minutes for *Lawrence* to come close enough for its 32-pdr carronades to reach an effective range. During that whole period it had to endure the fire of *Detroit*'s broadside – a ship with only two carronades. Now the moment has come for *Lawrence* to return what it is receiving. *Detroit* is a bare 60yd from *Lawrence*. At this point *Lawrence* has taken some damage, but nothing serious. Even if a ball from a long gun has the range to reach you, it has to hit to do damage – and the British gunners

seem to be having trouble aiming, as if their timing is off.

Lawrence has high bulwarks and a line of folded hammocks atop the bulwarks to protect the gunners, creating a head-high wall. Oliver Hazard Perry is standing on the bulwarks, to direct the battle. By standing atop the bulwarks, Perry can see *Detroit*'s hull, rather than just its masts and sail. For the next 90 minutes the crews of *Lawrence* and *Detroit* will be concentrating on just one task: loading, pointing, and firing their guns as fast as possible. At 50–60yd, you do not need to aim. Point the gun in the right direction, and fire. A degree or two – or more – of error does not matter.

QUARTERDECK VIEW: HMS *DETROIT*

It is 12:30pm, and Robert Heriot Barclay is satisfied with the progress of the battle. His sortie is a desperate throw of the dice. Unless he can beat the American squadron and regain control of Lake Erie, he is going to be starved out of his base. His gamble seems to be paying off, though. The Americans are attacking his squadron in detail. One American brig has sailed smack toward him, while the second brig, which should be fighting *Queen Charlotte*, seems to be hanging back. From the corner of his eye, Barclay can see the disengaged *Queen Charlotte* sailing to assist him. Perhaps he can knock out the nearer brig, the one flying a flag reading "DONT GIVE UP THE SHIP" before its companion can come to its assistance.

It is long odds. Barclay's ship is undermanned. The guns came from Fort Malden, providing a battery of such mixed types as to give a gunner nightmares. Most lack flintlocks. There are not even enough linstocks and slow match to go around. Some guns are being fired by flashing the lock of a pistol over the touchhole, which slows the rate of fire and makes aiming difficult for a trained gun captain — and Barclay has very few of those. It does not matter. The American brig is now well within musket range, inside 100yd, and closer to 50yd. At that range you fire and shoot. Long odds? For the last 50 years the Royal Navy has fought at a disadvantage and won.

As *Lawrence* crawled to within carronade range, it came under heavy fire. *Detroit*, unlike virtually every other ship on either side, had a battery of heavy long guns and could match *Lawrence*'s 24lb broadside with 120lb of iron. It was aided by *Chippawa*, which aimed its single 9-pdr long gun at the American flagship, ignoring the two leading schooners. For 20 minutes, until *Lawrence* drew close enough to *Detroit* for the carronades to be effective, *Lawrence* endured this superior fire. Finally, at 12:30pm, *Lawrence* was close enough. It opened up on *Detroit* with its carronades.

For the next 90 minutes the two ships exchanged broadsides. Casualties on both sides were heavy. Both sides were aiming at the hull, with the intent of knocking out the enemy's guns. Once *Lawrence* was within carronade range, the 32lb balls did substantial damage to *Detroit*'s bulwarks. The two lead US schooners also were in position to fire down the length of *Detroit*, their 12-pdr and 32-pdr long guns doing terrible damage. Yet the British were also doing terrible damage to *Lawrence*. By 1:30pm the ship's rigging had been so torn up by British shots which went high, it could no longer sail. The sailors and marines in the ship's fighting tops were called down to man the guns, to replace men previously wounded. Additionally, the raw American crews harmed their own efforts by overcharging their guns, several of which overturned as a result.

Nor by that time was *Lawrence* fighting *Detroit* the only engagement. Although *Niagara*'s cannonade put no pressure on *Queen Charlotte*, the long gun of the schooner *Somers* hurt the British vessel. *Niagara* and *Somers* concentrated on *Queen Charlotte*'s quarterdeck, and their fire soon killed Captain Robert Finnis, and wounded its first lieutenant, Mr. Stokoe. Command fell to Lieutenant Robert Irvine, of the Provincial Marine. Irvine realized *Queen Charlotte* was unable to effectually damage *Niagara* or *Somers* at long range, and could not close because his foe was upwind. On the other hand, he saw *Lawrence*, which *could* be brought within carronade range. To this end he had *Queen Charlotte* slip around *General Hunter*, and closed on *Lawrence*. Soon *Queen Charlotte*'s fire was also concentrated on *Lawrence*, at a range where its 24-pdr carronades were effective.

By 2:00pm most of *Lawrence*'s guns were out of action: dismounted due to overcharging, or having had breeching tackle cut and carriages knocked to pieces by enemy fire. Most of the crew was dead or wounded. (By battle's end, four-fifths of the crew was casualties.) The few survivors were reorganized to fire the remaining guns, which were aft. Yet *Lawrence* had dished out as much damage as it had received to the British ship-sloops. Neither was in as desperate a condition as *Lawrence* because *Lawrence* had spread its attentions over two ships, while *Lawrence* itself received the concentrated fire of *Detroit* and *Queen Charlotte*. Both British ships had lost enough rigging that they could only turn with the wind (wear) rather than turn into the wind (tack). They also had taken significant casualties.

And where was *Niagara*? Still behind *Caledonia* which, being much slower than *Lawrence*, allowed a gap to form in the American line. *Caledonia* continued to concentrate on *General Hunter*, gradually reducing its opponent to firewood. *Somers*, with the disappearance of *Queen Charlotte* had closed on the two trailing British warships, joining *Porcupine*, *Trippe*, and *Tigress* in battering *Lady Prevost* and *Little Belt*. Only *Niagara* was unengaged. *Niagara*'s behavior ultimately led to a court of inquiry over Jesse Elliott's conduct, and created a poisonous controversy which divided

By 2:30pm, *Lawrence* had been battered so badly only one of its guns was still capable of being fired. Perry personally aimed and fired the gun. By this point, fewer than a half-dozen men aboard *Lawrence*, including Perry, were uninjured. (LOC)

the US Navy for decades after the battle. Elliott insisted he had to maintain the line of battle. His detractors claimed he hung back due to cowardice or – perhaps worse – in hopes that Perry would be killed so Elliott could claim credit for victory.

The reason for Elliott's behavior may have been more prosaic. He was new to his command, having taken charge a bare month earlier, and his crew was raw. He may have lacked the ability to sail around *Caledonia*. Passing *Caledonia* on its unengaged side required tacking *Niagara*. In the light airs then present the attempt required a skilled crew and captain, for it risked having the ship end up "in irons" – trapped halfway through the maneuver, unable to complete it or fall back, and thus out of the battle. Sailing around the engaged side would have blocked *Caledonia*'s fire temporarily. Elliott, brave but unimaginative, apparently could find no solution other than play follow-my-leader with *Caledonia*.

Meanwhile, the situation aboard *Lawrence* continued to deteriorate. By 2:30pm not a single gun on the engaged side could be fired or worked. The marine lieutenant, one midshipman, and 20 other men were dead; 61 others were injured. Only 19 men were capable of fighting including the lightly injured. The sailing master and *Lawrence*'s two lieutenants told Perry the ship could no longer be fought. Perry agreed with the assessment, but was among the uninjured. He decided duty required him to continue the fight, even if his own ship could not.

BATTLE PHASE II: *NIAGARA* vs. *DETROIT*

Lawrence normally carried five ships' boats: two stowed over the main hold and three on davits at the ship's stern. In battle, ships' boats are a hazard; a shot hitting one would create splinters which could injure nearby men. When a ship cleared for action the boats were put overboard, sometimes towed behind a ship, or left behind with a few men aboard to tend the boats until the battle was over. *Lawrence* almost certainly towed her boats, because what happened next would have been impossible otherwise.

After *Lawrence*'s last functioning gun was fired, Perry decided to go to *Niagara*. He ordered the first cutter, one of two boats normally stored on deck, brought up to *Lawrence*. Once alongside, Perry turned over command of *Lawrence* to his first lieutenant, John Yarnell. Perry and four uninjured sailors boarded the cutter, and began rowing to *Niagara*. It was 2:30pm. Waiting 15 minutes after Perry left, until Perry reached *Niagara*, Yarnell, second lieutenant Dulaney Forest, and sailing master William Taylor decided further resistance was futile, and struck *Lawrence*'s colors.

Watching the flag lowered on *Lawrence* must have given Barclay satisfaction. The smaller ships of his little force were hurting. *General Hunter* was in poor shape. *Lady Prevost* had lost its rudder, and was falling to leeward. *Chippawa* and *Little Belt* were too weak to be consequential. *Detroit* had been hard hit, and its first lieutenant was mortally wounded. Barclay had been wounded twice in the duel with *Lawrence*: in the thigh and his remaining arm. *Queen Charlotte* was commanded by its junior lieutenant. Yet all the British ships were capable of being sailed, and were still in British hands. Neither *Caledonia* nor the six American schooners could face the two ship-sloops, and the remaining 20-gun brig was virtually inert. All that remained to secure victory was to take possession of the surrendered *Lawrence* and escape to Amherstburg. *Detroit* and *Queen Charlotte* were powerful enough to command Lake Erie against the rest of the US Navy squadron even if *Lawrence* could not be repaired. With victory apparently in hand, Barclay finally allowed himself to be taken below to be treated by the surgeon.

Meanwhile, Perry completed the boat voyage to *Niagara*. The wind began strengthening while Perry was making his way from *Lawrence* to *Niagara*. As a result, *Niagara* was now setting its furled topgallant sails and shaking out its mainsail. Seeing this, the British assumed *Niagara* was preparing to run. Perry instead renewed the engagement. He took command of *Niagara*, giving Elliott his boat, and instructions to go to the four trailing schooners and urge them forward. Elliott may not have been able to get *Niagara* moving, but Perry did. He put the helm down, sailed inside *Caledonia*, and headed for the slow-moving *Detroit*. In a few minutes he passed the motionless *Lawrence*. It served as a general signal to Perry's force. *Ariel* and *Scorpion* turned to engage *Chippawa*. The four trailing schooners turned on *General Hunter* and *Queen Charlotte*.

Niagara was sailing with the wind on its quarter. Five minutes later it was 60yd from *Detroit*, then under the command of Lieutenant George Inglis, and turned on a parallel course. *Detroit* opened fire as *Niagara* began sailing past, but much of the British vessel's crew was dead or seriously injured, those who remained on deck were exhausted, and several guns were out of action. Several shots struck *Niagara*; they had some effect, but not nearly enough to cause serious damage. Five of *Niagara*'s crew were killed or mortally wounded, and another 21 were wounded during the battle. Most of these casualties occurred at this point in the battle, while *Detroit* could reach *Niagara*.

As *Niagara* began pulling ahead of *Detroit*, Inglis must have realized to his horror that Perry was trying to rake *Detroit*. Perry planned to place *Niagara* perpendicular to *Detroit* across its bow. That would allow *Niagara*'s entire broadside to hit *Detroit*, while *Detroit* would only be able to respond with its bow pivot. The 32lb balls from *Niagara*'s carronades would run the length of *Detroit*, tripling or quadrupling the damage they would do.

Perry's boat voyage to *Niagara* became legendary; the subject of numerous, generally inaccurate paintings. In reality, only four sailors accompanied Perry in the boat, with Perry probably at the tiller, instead of dramatically gesturing. (LOC)

Detroit was close-hauled to the wind. If it turned to port it would end up in irons. As *Niagara* moved to cross *Detroit*'s bow, Inglis wore *Detroit* to starboard, keeping *Niagara* on his beam. The two ships were separated by no more than a few dozen yards. *Niagara* was hammering *Detroit*. By this point *Detroit* had taken so much damage, one Provincial Marine officer later claimed it would have been impossible to place a hand on *Detroit*'s side without laying the hand upon a shot hole.

OVERLEAF: *NIAGARA* vs. *DETROIT*

By 2:55pm *Lawrence* was out of the fight, but Perry was not. He shifted his flag to *Niagara* and has sailed it to fight both British ship-sloops. He has finally come abeam *Detroit*. The two ships have begun trading broadsides at a range where every shot will hit – except that *Niagara*'s crew is fresh, and its battery undamaged, while the men aboard *Detroit* have been fighting for nearly two hours and their ship is badly damaged. Meanwhile, *Queen Charlotte* is too far away for its guns to be effective. Nor can *Detroit* receive assistance from any ship other than *Queen Charlotte*. *Lady Prevost* and *Little Belt* are out of the fight. *Chippawa* has its hands full fighting two schooners. *General Hunter* is hard pressed by the trailing American schooners. *Lawrence* has been battered to a standstill and is simply drifting, its colors struck and fewer than 20 uninjured men left aboard. It is out of the fight. *Niagara*, like *Detroit*, is close-hauled to the wind. It cannot sail much closer to the direction of the wind, but it does not need to. It is sailing parallel to *Detroit*, and sailing faster than *Detroit*. In a few minutes it will be ahead of *Detroit*, in a position to place itself across *Detroit*'s bows. If it is allowed to do that, the battle will be lost for the British. Yet, *Detroit* cannot turn to starboard without exposing itself to a raking broadside from *Niagara*. The climax of the battle is at hand.

The battle ended after *Detroit* and *Queen Charlotte* locked yardarms, allowing *Niagara* to place itself in a position to rake both British vessels. *Queen Charlotte* struck its colors first, soon followed by *Detroit*. This painting is in a federal courthouse in Cleveland, Ohio. (LOC)

Meanwhile, *Queen Charlotte* was a spectator because Perry's approach put *Niagara* out of the effective range of *Queen Charlotte*'s carronades. All Lieutenant Irvine could do was watch the duel between *Niagara* and *Detroit*. Then he saw an opportunity as *Niagara* began passing *Detroit*. If *Queen Charlotte* put the helm down, and turned 30 degrees to starboard, it might be possible to place his ship where it could rake *Niagara*. If *Niagara* turned away from *Queen Charlotte*, it would expose its stern to *Detroit*. *Queen Charlotte* wore. Unfortunately, even with the freshening breeze, *Queen Charlotte* moved too slowly for the attempt to succeed. Instead, it sailed in front of *Detroit*'s bow, with the result that *Detroit* was forced to veer sharply to starboard to avoid *Queen Charlotte*. The two ships ended up locking yardarms port side to port side. Locked together, the two ships could only wait, immobile, as Perry brought *Niagara* across *Detroit*'s stern and *Queen Charlotte*'s bow.

The situation for the British was hopeless; the result inevitable. The two British ships managed to disentangle themselves, but neither could continue the battle or run. First *Queen Charlotte* struck its colors. Then Inglis ordered *Detroit*'s flag struck. Perry boarded *Detroit* to accept its surrender. The rest of the British squadron soon followed suit. *Lady Prevost* was unmanageable. *General Hunter* was surrounded by four American schooners. *Chippawa* was being double-teamed by *Ariel* and *Scorpion*. *Little Belt* had fallen astern. *Little Belt* might have stolen away, but to what purpose? All four struck their colors. It was shortly before 3:15pm. Lake Erie now belonged to the United States.

STATISTICS AND ANALYSIS

The Battle of Lake Erie created two cottage industries. One, made up mostly of British and Canadian writers (starting with William James in the immediate postwar years), attempts to prove Barclay was doomed from the start and his defeat and US victory were inevitable. The other, springing from American authors, has written reams demonstrating how the battle was a close-run thing, with US victory secured only by the presence of Oliver Hazard Perry. A strong case can be made that both sides are right and talking past each other.

Strictly measured by broadside and manpower, the US force had a clear edge. While the British ships mounted more guns, the US guns were significantly heavier. In both long guns and carronades, the US force carried a larger broadside than the British – in terms of weight of metal thrown, almost double that of the British. While a 2.46:1 superiority in carronade broadside contributed to the US advantage, even counting the broadside thrown by long guns, the US force overmatched the British by one-eighth.

The US superiority, especially in long guns, was spread among a large number of vessels with a small number of guns. Seven US vessels mounting four or fewer guns provided a long-gun broadside weight of 216lb, almost equal to the British long-gun broadside weight of 222lb. Yet if we examine the two largest ships on each side, *Lawrence* and *Niagara* and *Detroit* and *Queen Charlotte*, US superiority becomes even clearer. Each US brig threw a broadside of 300lb, almost as much as the total broadside of the two British ship-sloops combined.

British long-gun superiority through *Detroit* was largely nullified even at long range. The lack of flintlocks meant its rate of fire would be slow. More importantly,

OVERLEAF Perry's decision to continue the action in *Niagara* reversed what was developing into a US defeat and British victory into an overwhelming US victory – the most complete defeat the Royal Navy ever suffered, with every British ship present captured. (LOC)

69

the lack of trained gunners meant most long-range shots would miss. Sloops-of-war were generally armed with carronades because (except in rare instances) ships had to be within 50yd to reasonably expect to hit anything. A ship-of-the-line, with scores of guns firing on a broadside, expected a few to land. A sloop-of-war, with a dozen or less, could expect one hit – if it was lucky.

United States gunnery strength				
Ship name	Guns mounted	Broadside weight (lb)		
		Long guns	Carronades	Total
Lawrence[1]	20	24	288	312
Niagara	20	12	288	300
Ariel[2]	4	48	0	48
Caledonia[2]	3	24	18	42
Scorpion[2]	2	32	32	64
Somers[2]	2	24	24	48
Tigress[2]	2	32	0	32
Porcupine[2]	1	32	0	32
Trippe[2]	1	24	0	24
Total	55	252	650	902

1. Mounted both 12-pdrs on the engaged side.   2. All guns in pivot mounts.

Royal Navy gunnery strength				
Ship name	Guns mounted	Broadside weight (lb)		
		Long guns	Carronades	Total
Detroit[1]	19	114	24	138
Queen Charlotte[2]	17	48	168	216
Lady Prevost[3]	13	18	60	78
General Hunter	10	18	12	30
Little Belt	3	15	0	15
Chippawa[4]	1	9	0	9
Total	63	222	264	486

1. One 18-pdr long gun on a pivot.   2. One 24-pdr long gun on a pivot.
3. One 9-pdr long gun on a pivot.   4. Pivot mount.

The sides were more evenly matched when it came to manpower. Perry had 532 men entered on the rolls of his ships, although on the day of battle 116 were on the sick list, too ill to fight. This gave Perry 416 effectives, of which 131 were on *Lawrence* and 140 were on *Niagara*. The exact number of men aboard the British ships is unknown because the muster rolls were lost with the battle. Roosevelt, in his book *The Naval War of 1812*, estimates British manpower at between 440 and 490 men, giving Barclay a slight superiority in numbers. Of these, *Detroit* had 150 and *Queen Charlotte*

WHY WERE CARRONADES SO SHORT RANGED?

At 5 degrees elevation, a 9-pdr long gun's range was 1,600yd. A 32-pdr carronade could reach 1,200yd. Yet 9-pdrs could reliably hit a target at 150yd, while carronades were ineffective beyond 50yd. The reason may lie in a combination of poor training and the carronade's geometry, not inherent carronade inaccuracy.

The carronade was narrower at the muzzle than at the breech. Aiming a carronade by sighting along the top of the gun meant the carronade's bore pointed 4 degrees higher than the target aimed at. The ball followed a trajectory significantly higher than intended. At 100yd, it would be over 20ft higher – enough to fly completely over the hull of the targeted ship.

The crews of both sides were ill-trained and unpracticed, especially the British crews. Many were firing their guns for the first time. The result was that carronade-armed ships, especially *Queen Charlotte*, were effectively out of the battle at ranges greater than 50yd.

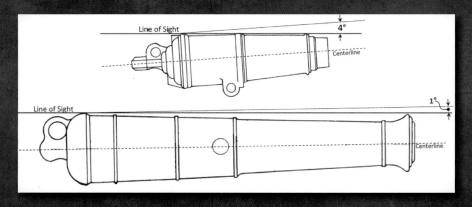

The bore of a carronade was misaligned with a sight line along the top of the barrel by 4 degrees, ensuring the shot would fly high unless compensation for the bias was made. (AC)

between 120 and 130. In other words, the two biggest vessels on both sides had roughly the same number of men split between them.

The biggest difference between the two sides lay largely in the quality of men each possessed. Barclay had no more than 70 men who could be rated as ordinary and able seamen. Perry had roughly 100 to 120 men in these categories. Since these had to be split among nine ships instead of Barclay's six, the sides were roughly equally matched, with the United States taking a slight edge.

US superiority did not automatically doom the British, who had fought other battles against longer odds and won. Against the United States, the battle most often went to the side with the heavier broadside, but Barclay had to fight or fold. He came extremely close to victory, through fighting his foe in detail. The combined firepower of *Detroit* and *Queen Charlotte* exceeded that of any one US brig, and for most of the battle, that is how Barclay fought.

The battle started out as ship-to-ship duels between *Lawrence* and *Detroit* and between *Niagara* and *Queen Charlotte*. *Detroit* had the advantage in the long-gun duel with *Lawrence*. Shortly after *Lawrence* closed to carronade range, *Detroit* was joined by *Queen Charlotte*. *Niagara*, by failing to close range with *Queen Charlotte*, allowed the ship-sloop to slip away from an ineffectual bow-chaser match to where it could materially aid *Detroit*. *Lawrence* and *Detroit* battered each other into wrecks. *Queen Charlotte*, farther from *Lawrence*, was at the edge of the effective range of its carronades, but helped reduce *Lawrence*.

HMS *Royal George* escapes from US gunboats on Lake Ontario. *Royal George* was a near-sister ship to *Detroit* and *Queen Charlotte*. (AC)

Why *Queen Charlotte* failed to close range, the puzzle of *Niagara*'s inaction in the opening phase of the battle, and the inability of *Queen Charlotte* to avoid falling foul of *Detroit* at the end of the battle share a common root cause. All of the ships, British and US, had green crews. The US brigs had been manned for just over a month. In order to man *Detroit*, Barclay had shifted crews around. He also replaced *Queen Charlotte*'s original captain with Robert Finnis, a Royal Navy officer sent from Lake Ontario.

The captains of the four biggest sloops-of-war were unfamiliar with the peculiarities of their ships. So were the sailors manning the ships. They were competent enough under ordinary circumstances, but the battle was fought under light airs with baffling winds. A crew which had worked together for three to six months, with a captain who had pushed his ship to its limits under a variety of circumstances, would have been up to the challenge the wind created. Tacking in light winds with the shallow, saucer-shaped hulls of Lakes warships required outstanding seamanship. A moment's inattention – one sailor hauling the wrong line or loosing the wrong reef point – could leave a ship attempting to turn across the wind stalled, "in irons" and unable to turn or move. It could take as much as 30 minutes to turn the ship where it could catch the wind, leaving it at the mercy of the enemy until then.

Barclay understood the limitations under which he acted. He did not attempt to close on Perry's force by tacking to gain the upwind position because his crews were not up to the effort. Instead, he sailed as close to the wind as he could without risking losing momentum. So did Finnis, and his successor, Lieutenant Irvine of *Queen Charlotte*. Irvine slipped behind *General Hunter* to close with *Lawrence*. Similarly, Perry and Elliott never attempted to tack, closing on the British ships with simple

maneuvers, relying on the wind on their port quarter to move their ships to close with the British. Once *Queen Charlotte* slipped away from *Niagara*, Elliott was baffled. He could not follow *Queen Charlotte* and was unwilling to sail between *Caledonia* and its target. Perry, on the other hand, focused on the overall goal. He sailed straight at the enemy, whether aboard *Lawrence* or, later, on *Niagara*.

Perry's willingness to grapple with the enemy and unwillingness to concede the battle while he had means to fight was the ultimate reason the United States won. Had Perry not taken command of *Niagara*, Barclay would have won the battle despite *Detroit*'s severe damage. Furthermore, Perry's swift approach forced the inexperienced lieutenants commanding *Detroit* and *Queen Charlotte* into maneuvers beyond their capacities. Although *Niagara* could have eventually battered *Queen Charlotte* into submission, the collision between the two British ships effectively ended the battle.

That the crews were inexperienced did not mean they were unwilling to fight. Both sides stood to their guns until they no longer had guns to work. Although the gunners were inexperienced, they fought at ranges where they could not miss. At the end of the battle, of the 103 fit men originally aboard *Lawrence*, 22 were dead and 61 wounded. Only 20 were uninjured, capable of fighting. In all, 27 men were killed and 96 wounded aboard Perry's ships. While Barclay did not tally casualties by ship, he reported 41 killed and 94 wounded. Given the disparity of result, the butcher's bill was remarkably balanced.

AFTERMATH

At twilight, the bodies of the dead, except for six officers, were consigned to the waters of Lake Erie. The British prizes and the United States vessels returned to Put-in-Bay, and anchored. On September 11, both sides participated in a joint funeral service for the officers slain during the battle: three British and three American. *Detroit* and *Queen Charlotte* were converted to hospital ships to treat the many sick and wounded. Over the next few weeks Perry used the least-damaged prizes and ships to ferry Harrison's army to Canada. On October 5, Harrison would beat a British army led by Brigadier-General Henry Proctor at the Battle of the Thames (or Moraviantown). Any threat to the United States' Northwest Territories was over, although Britain still held Fort Michilimackinac.

Perry quitted Lake Erie in October, turning command over to Elliott. Both decided to leave Lake Huron for 1814. Elliott's tenure was ill-starred. He let Erie run down and wintered most of the schooners at Black Rock, where they were trapped and burned by the British. Chauncey sent Captain Arthur Sinclair to command the Upper Lakes, but he did as poorly as had Elliott. He failed to take Fort Michilimackinac and lost two more schooners, captured by the British. These losses did not change the balance of power on the Upper Lakes, however –the US Navy was too strong.

The Lakes warships of both sides vanished soon after the war ended. The 1816 Rush–Bagot Treaty disarmed the Great Lakes, limiting both sides to two warships: one for the Upper Lakes and one for Lake Ontario. Most of the large sloops-of-war, including *Detroit*, *Queen Charlotte*, and *Lawrence*, were submerged to preserve them against a need which never came. *Niagara* became a receiving ship; the rest were sold back to merchant service.

The War of 1812 ended with perhaps the best outcome for both nations: stalemate; a peace dictating a return to status quo ante, with no territory lost or gained by either nation. The end of the Napoleonic Wars ended Britain's need to impress sailors for the

Royal Navy and blockade US trade. Britain never abjured impressment or blockade in the peace treaty, but peace made both a dead letter. Never again would the United States seek Canada, for territorial ambitions toward Canada came at a higher price than the new nation was willing to pay. Balancing this against the potential dismemberment of the United States should the fortunes of war go badly meant the risks were higher than any possible return. The United States was well pleased to end the war intact.

Nor would the United States and Great Britain ever go to war again. They came close a few times: the Mackenzie Rebellion in 1837–38, the Oregon boundary dispute in 1845, and the American Civil War of 1861–65. Instead, they became allies in the 20th century. The Canadian–United States border became the longest unfortified border in the world, while Britain and the United States maintained a "special relationship" which spanned the century.

The bell of *Queen Charlotte* was subsequently used on *Niagara*. Later, the captured bell was given to the city of Erie, Pennsylvania. For many years it hung in City Hall, but is now on display at the Erie Maritime Museum. (AC)

FURTHER READING

There are a remarkable number of books about the war on the Lakes in the War of 1812, especially the Battle of Lake Erie. There was a flurry of works which came out for the centennial and bicentennial of the war, some of which were excellent. Others were patriotic tub-thumpers, fun to read but not necessarily reliable. Peeling away mythology to expose the underlying facts is an author's challenge.

Two recent works I would recommend wholeheartedly are *Warships of the Great Lakes 1754–1834* by Robert Malcomson (Annapolis, MD: Naval Institute Press, 2001), and *Coffins of the Brave: Lake Shipwrecks of the War of 1812*, edited by Kevin Crisman (College Station, TX: Texas A&M University Press, 2014). While the Battle of Lake Erie is not the focus of either book, both offer superior insights on the construction and operation of the ships used in the battle.

If you are seeking another perspective on the battle, read *The Lake Erie Campaign of 1813: I Shall Fight Them This Day*, by Walter Rybka (Charleston, SC: The History Press, 2012). Rybka is Program Director for the Erie Maritime Museum and captain of the US Brig *Niagara* which sails out of the museum. He knows his stuff.

I tended to use original sources to the extent I could. There is a wealth of information in books printed in the 19th and early 20th centuries which include memoirs by or papers of participants, court-martial records, and other official documentation. Many are now available online via archive.org (these are marked with an asterisk in the bibliography). These also include later sources such as the US Navy's various documentary histories which include the three-volume *The Naval War of 1812: A Documentary History*, edited by William S. Dudley (Washington, DC: Naval Historical Center, Department of the Navy, 1965). Other sources include:

Caney, Donald L., *Sailing Warships of the US Navy* (Annapolis, MD: US Naval Institute Press, 2001).

Chapelle, Howard I., *The History of the American Sailing Navy* (New York, NY: W.W. Norton, 1949).

Dobbins, Daniel & William W. Dobbins, "The Dobbins Papers," *Publications of the Buffalo Historical Society, Vol. VIII* (Buffalo, NY: Buffalo Historical Society, 1905).*

Douglas, Howard, *A Tretise on Naval Gunnery*, 2nd Ed. (London: John Murray, 1829).*

Harland, John, *Seamanship in the Age of Sail* (Annapolis, MD: Naval Institute Press, 1990).

Mahan, Alfred T., *Sea Power In Its Relations To The War Of 1812*, two vols (London: S. Low, Marston & Co., 1905).*

Paullin, Charles Oscar, *The Battle of Lake Erie: A Collection of Documents, chiefly by Commodore Perry: including the Court-martial of Commander Barclay and the Court of Enquiry on Captain Elliott* (Cleveland, OH: The Rowfant Club, 1918).*

"Perry's Victory Centennial Number," *The Journal of American History*, First Quarter 1914, Vol. VIII (January–February–March), No. 1.*

Roosevelt, Theodore, *The Naval War of 1812* (New York, NY & London: G.P. Putnam's Sons, 1900).*

Tucker, Spencer, *Arming the Fleet: U.S. Navy Ordnance in the Muzzle-Loading Era* (Annapolis, MD: Naval Institute Press, 1989).

The US Navy commemorated the Battle of Lake Erie by naming a Ticonderoga-class guided missile cruiser for it. USS *Lake Erie* is a test ship for the US Theater-Wide Ballistic Missile Defense Program. Its accomplishments include shooting down the malfunctioning United States reconnaissance satellite USA-193 from orbit on February 21, 2008. (USNHHC)

INDEX